SPEEDWAY LEGENDS

For McSkid and The Norwich Nut

Without them none of this would have been possible.
And both of them know who they are.

First published in Great Britain in 2015
Copyright © John Chaplin and John Somerville 2015

A CIP record for this title is available from the British Library

ISBN 978 0 85704 271 2

HALSGROVE
Halsgrove House,
Ryelands Business Park,
Bagley Road, Wellington, Somerset TA21 9PZ
Tel: 01823 653777   Fax: 01823 216796
email: sales@halsgrove.com

Part of the Halsgrove group of companies.
Information on all Halsgrove titles is available at: www.halsgrove.com

Printed in China by Everbest Printing Co Ltd

SPEEDWAY LEGENDS

WITH A FOREWORD BY LEN SILVER

CHAPLIN AND SOMERVILLE

HALSGROVE

BY THE SAME AUTHORS

JOHN CHAPLIN:

Wings And Space: History Of Aviation

Speedway: The Story of The World Championship

John Chaplin's Speedway Special: The Classic Legends

Ove Fundin Speedway Superstar

Tom Farndon: The Greatest Speedway Rider Of Them All with Norman Jacobs

Ivan Mauger: The Man Behind the Myth

Speedway Superheroes with John Somerville

Speedway: The Greatest Moments with John Somerville

Main Dane: My Story by Hans Nielsen (Edit, production, design)

History of the Speedway Hoskins by Ian Hoskins (Edit, production, design)

A Fistful of Twistgrip

Vintage Speedway Magazine (Founder, Editor, Publisher)

JOHN SOMERVILLE:

Speedway Times Past with Howard Jones

The Illustrated History of 100 British Speedway Tracks with Howard Jones

Kiwi Kings of Speedway

Speedway Superheroes with John Chaplin

Speedway: The Greatest Moments with John Chaplin

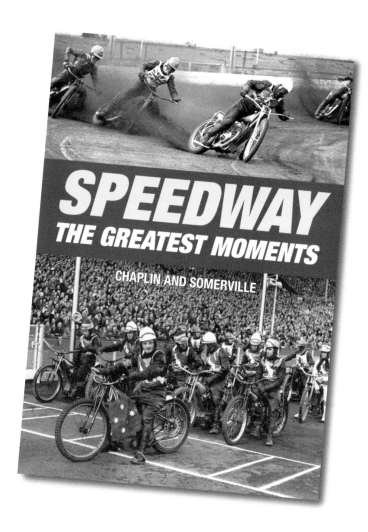

WHAT THEY SAID ABOUT
Speedway – The Greatest Moments

Immensely readable … the photographs are special.

– Peter Oakes, Speedway Star

The book is absolutely great. I'll say it again, JUST GREAT.

– Nick Nicolaides, captain of the
American speedway team in the 1950s

John Chaplin is outstanding among speedway journalists for style and his brilliant writing. Speedway owes a debt to John Somerville for preserving its history in pictures.

– Dave Lanning

Chaplin and Somerville are a formidable team. Chaplin must now be placed alongside the sport's greatest writers. Somerville's wonderful pictures are of equal value to Chaplin's prose.

– Speedway Plus website

CONTENTS

AUTHORS' NOTE

John Chaplin

John Somerville

THIS BOOK, the third in a trilogy by the John Chaplin/John Somerville partnership, is called *Speedway Legends*. It is inspired by and based on a series of features we contributed for some years to *Classic Speedway Magazine*.

The accolade *Legend*, to describe recent or vintage sports stars, is used often far too readily and frequently these days. It is not always earned, or merited.

However, the line-up we have here is a unique assembly of real and genuine legends of speedway – at least in our opinion. One in particular, the truly legendary *(he's certainly earned it)* promoter Len Silver, has graciously agreed to write the foreword. *Thanks Uncle Len.*

It is by no means a definitive record of the sport's legends: there are not enough books and not enough time to do justice to them all. You will certainly have your own ideas of who they are ... and we have probably left out your special favourite anyway.

It is an attempt to honour the many personalities we particularly admire and to make speedway enthusiasts aware of how their contribution to the development of the sport has made it what it is today.

Among the many who have helped with the compilation of this whole series are: Henrik Andersen, Brian Bott, Brian Buck, Brian Burford, Richard Clark, Scott Dalosio, Kelly Dinardo, James Easter, Bruce Flanders, Ove Fundin, Bert Harkins, Mike Kemp, Tomasz Lorek, Stephen Magro, Ronnie Moore, Shani Moore, Nick Nicolaides, Peter Oakes, Jan Ossowscy, Jarek Pabijan, John Parker, Mike Patrick, Mark Plummer, Maggie Radcliffe, Gary Roberts, Peter Sampson, Craig Saul, Diana Sharkey (née Clarke), Andrew Skeels, Mark Warren, Tony Webb, Peter White, Howie 'Hard Hat' Zechner.

We would like to send a big thank you to every one of them, and special thanks to Steven Pugsley and Denise Lyons at Halsgrove.

John Chaplin and John Somerville

FOREWORD

Len receives his Lifetime Achievement Award from former World Champion Ove Fundin.

JOHN CHAPLIN and I grew up with speedway. We are about the same age, though I am just a bit senior to him. While I went legitimate and made the switch from cycle speedway to the real thing in the 1950s and then into promoting, John made the switch from cycle speedway – he boasted to me that he was once the Hall Green Match Race Champion – and went into journalism.

I have always enjoyed his style of writing, and there is no doubt that his contribution to the sport over the years has been considerable because in that time his publicity value must have run into millions of pounds. His dedication to preserving speedway history is well known and respected throughout the speedway world and this book is his latest effort. I certainly hope it won't be the last from him and his collaborator John Somerville.

I didn't really get to know John until his son Christopher rode for me first in the Hackney Junior team and then at Rye House. He was never afraid to get down and dirty in the pits on race night, which was about as close as he could be to the sport without actually riding. Not many journalists are prepared to do that. So I was pleased to write a series of articles for his *Vintage Speedway Magazine* on how I prepared the Wembley World Final tracks.

We both do our best to publicise speedway and I remember well that after Rye House closed he promised to eat his hat if it ever opened again. Well, I made sure that speedway did return to Rye House and John duly arrived with a 'hat' he'd had specially made out of sponge cake and kept his promise to eat it in front of the first night crowd.

Soon after that he bribed me with a bottle of champagne to get back on a bike after forty years. I rode just one lap but I was happy to go along with it even though it was all a publicity stunt for his magazine. He is the only journalist I would have done that for.

Below left: *Chaplin eats hat on reopening night at Rye House.*

Below right: *Len with his boys: Adam Roynon (left) and super Rocket 2013 World Champion Tai Woffinden.*

John's partner in this book is John Somerville, whose archive of historic speedway pictures is unique. The images he has collected are just as important as the Chaplin words – though some say more important because isn't a picture supposed to be worth more than a thousand words? Their two previous efforts, *Speedway Superheroes* and *Speedway: The Greatest Moments*, were brilliant and I know every speedway fan, including me, will enjoy this book about the sport's legends … by two legends – Chaplin and Somerville – in their own right.

Len Silver
Rye House Speedway 2015

Performing for his Hackney crowd, promoter Len (always) puts on a show.

YOUNG SAM'S EPIC RIDE

THIS LITTLE GEM is a whimsical item to get things off to what Chaplin and Somerville hope will be a pleasurable experience. It appeared in the *Belle Vue Bulletin* of 23 October, 1948, the last match of the season and Belle Vue's 696th meeting.

It is based on a comic monolgue made famous by the renowned music hall comedian Stanley Augustus Holloway OBE which was about Sam Small, a lowly musketeer in Wellington's army, who dropped his rifle on parade before the Battle of Waterloo and refused to pick it up until asked, *nicely*, by the Duke himself.

The Cast:
    SAM SMALL
    MISS HART (Alice Hart the Belle Vue manager)

The Belle Vue team:
    JACK PARKER (CAPTAIN)
    JIM BOYD
    WALLY HULL
    BILL PITCHER

DENT OLIVER
JACK CHIGNELL
WALLY LLOYD
LOUIS LAWSON

Special Guest stars:
    FRANK VAREY (pre-war Belle Vue Ace)
    RON CLARKE (Odsal Boomerangs captain)
    OLIVER HART (Odsal Boomerangs team member)

Aces on parade. The cast from left: Wally Lloyd, Jim Boyd, Walter Hull, Bill Pitcher, John Deeley manager, Jack Parker on bike, Louis Lawson, Bill Rogers, Jack Chignell, Dent Oliver.

You've heard of the Wars Of The Roses
Of the Aces and Boomerangs too
Well here is a tale that you've not heard about
So now I will tell it to you
You know young Sam Small who created a stir
With Wellington down at the 'Loo
When he was demobbed he was going to ride
For the Aces at dear old Belle Vue

He asked for a trial and was really quite good
But Jack Parker got Sam on the mat
He wanted young Sam to ride at reserve
Said Sam: I'm not standing for that
So Sam went off and looked up Miss Hart
And explained to her about t'bother
And said: If you think I should ride at reserve
Well I'm not so you'd best get another

So Jack got the boys all together
And as all around him they stood
He said: You've seen Sam out there on the track
You'll admit that he's really quite good
Oh quite, said Jim Boyd, while Louis just grinned
And Wally didn't know where to look
Wally Lloyd and Bill Pitcher both puffed on their pipes
Dent and Chiggy just opened a book

Now look here, said Jack, I need all your help
For this problem we've got to decide
'Cos someone will have to sit here in the pits
While Sam goes out there for his ride
Said Dent: That's OK let him team up with me
But Wally Lloyd turned that down flat:
If you think I'll stop here or ride at reserve
I too am not standing for that

Said Louis: Hey Wally Hull what about you?
You're as ancient as ancient can be
But Wally said: Nay lad, I'm not standing down
And Bill said: And that goes for me
Said Jack: Now really you don't expect me
I'm not Match Race Champion for nowt
I just couldn't stand down so you'll have to think twice
'Cos that idea's definitely out

Jim Boyd and Jack Chignell argued with Jack
And neither could see any reason
Why they should stand down to let young Sam ride
On the very last night of the season
As the meeting went on the excitement grew tense
All the boys had ideas that were wary
When into the pits came a chap they all knew
He was known to them all as Frank Varey

When they explained to Frank he laughed loud and long
And said: It's easy to see
Young Sam's got you all where he wants you
Now look here, just leave him to me
So when Saturday came round, the Aces came out
Johnnie Hoskins's Boomerang too
And there in the pits was Frank Varey
And the stadium was packed at Belle Vue

Young Sam was there 'cos he'd got his own way
Though the Aces were wondering who
Was going to stand down and let young Sam ride
But Frank Varey just grinned 'cos he knew
Jack and Wally came out and sprang into the lead
And stayed there for two or three laps
But while they both worried about young Sam Small
Ron Clarke put it over our chaps

Bill and Louis came out, and both wore a frown
For they hadn't the least idea who
Would sit in the pits to make way for young Sam
And that's how we lost Heat two
After Heat three when Dent had a go
Oliver Hart had some reason for glee
For he beat Dent and Wally – they were second and third
So that made the score three-three

Then after Heat four young Sam said to all
Well now I've the track to myself
Frank said I could ride, and by gum he was right
So I needn't be left on the shelf
Sam winked at Frank and stepped out onto the track
And the crowd raised the roof with a roar
For they knew that young Sam was the best in the land
And he'd soon make a change to the score

As he strode down the track all the fans gave a cheer
And young Sam had a smile on his face
He said to himself: I'll just do my bit
Then the Aces will win every race
As the boys stood around getting set for Heat five
They all had a look at the track
They stared and they gaped, and then they all grinned
And each one slapped t'other on t'back

They laughed loud and long, as they stared out at Sam
For they'd all missed one vital factor
'Cos Sam was out there as proud as could be
He was grading the track on the tractor

Walter 'Wally' Green

HOW WALLY GREEN FOUND SALVATION

THE SPORTING and military education of Walter 'Wally' Green included, he admitted: 'How I learned that no one picks up fallen exhaust pipes; how to rake a cinder track; how to owe Dick Case £1; what happens when you lose 34 Army lorries; how to get rejected by every London speedway plus Arsenal Football Club, and how to fall off at the first bend at West Ham…'

However, Wally finally did find salvation: first at the very bottom of the speedway world with veteran Charlie Dugard's Division Three speedway team at Eastbourne, and then at just one place from the top of the speedway world on a magic World Final night at Wembley.

It was like this.

Wally said: 'I delivered greengrocery to a Mrs Day in Finchley and she gave me my usual glass of lemonade. I was wearing my Wembley speedway supporter's badge and she asked me if I ever went to the track at Boreham Wood where her husband, Mr Alan Day, promoted on Sundays. If I'd like to go there, she said, she thought Mr Day would find me a job.

'The following Sunday I cycled the six miles there and was not only welcomed by Mr Day, but given a rake and allowed to go onto the track. This was fantastic for a lad of twelve years of age. The original grass track was slowly being covered with cinders that came from the local gas works. We had to get there one hour before the start of the meeting to spread the cinders over the grass from the piles that were unloaded from a horse and cart. When Mr Day, who was promoter, AC-U steward (referee), starter and cashier, was satisfied, the riders came out and did a couple of warm-up laps.

'Two things stood out in my memory about that first day as a raker. Firstly I saw Lionel Van Praag walking around the pits. For a Wembley supporter like me, that was incredible.

On the way up: Wally is presented with a trophy at Rye House by his West Ham captain-to-be Eric Chitty … but their relationship was not always full of smiles.

Secondly, in one race an exhaust pipe fell off a bike and lay in the middle of the track. The other rakers did nothing about it, but so that the riders wouldn't hit it when they came round again, with great bravery I ran out and picked it up … and I found out why the other rakers had left it there.

'Among the better riders were Percy Brine, George Wilks, Tommy Price (*See Page 90*) and Archie Windmill. They all went on to be top class professionals, Tommy as World Champion.

'As I cycled home to Finchley, I decided that one day I would become a speedway rider. Little did I realise that many years later I would ride against George Wilks and Tommy Price at Wembley.

'My job as a trainee gas fitter meant I'd had to buy a bicycle which was useful to get me to Wembley speedway every Thursday. I bought one from Gamages in Holborn on hire purchase. It cost me £2 and I paid half a crown (12.5pence) each week.

One of my fellow apprentices had an old Douglas motorcycle. But after an accident with a car he swapped it with me for my pushbike. I was then 17 with my own motorbike and was speedway mad.

'I marked out a track in a nearby field, but a man who stopped me suggested I went to a place called Rye House where they had a speedway track and I could make all the noise I liked.

'Training was carried out by Dicky Case, the famous Australian international, who charged £1 for four laps, so I started to save half a crown each week. On the last day of August 1939 I went back to Rye House with my £1 and was allowed to have four laps. The thrill of those four laps was terrific and Dicky suggested I should have another pound's worth. But as I would have had to save up again he let me owe him the pound and I did another four laps.

'He called me over as I was leaving and said: "Come back next week. I think I know where I could get you some rides for nothing."

'But before that could happen war was declared on September 3 and I went off into the Army for the next seven years. Of the 440 men in my unit only eight could drive. Four of us had motorcycles and we were sent home by bus to collect them. We were then classed as Dispatch Riders and paid an extra shilling (5 pence) a day plus another sixpence (2.5 pence) for using our own motorbikes.

'Lorries and drivers were hired from a local haulage company and our convoy left from Wimbledon to go to Bletchley. I was the leading dispatch rider and had never heard of Bletchley. At each junction we lost a few vehicles, some went over Putney bridge instead of along the South Circular Road and when we arrived at what is now Brent Cross I was alone.

'So I went home to Finchley where my mother cooked me egg and chips. My father said I should be shot for deserting my convoy in time of war. The Army decided I was useless on a motorcycle and withdrew my 1s 6d a day. They then put me in charge of a gun and put me on a troopship to the Western Desert. I remained there for a very long time as punishment for losing 34 lorries in Wandsworth.

'In 1946 I became an instructor at Hendon Technical College. This was not very exciting so I wrote many letters offering my services to several sporting organizations including Arsenal Football Club and all the London speedway tracks. To my great disappointment only Wembley and New Cross replied, and they both rejected me.'

The letter from Wembley was dated 20 April 1947 and read:

'Dear Sir,

In reply to your letter, I regret I cannot help you. We have now completed our training scheme at Rye House having secured all the riders we can possibly handle for the coming season.
 I understand West Ham Speedway, Custom House, London E.16 are organizing trials in the near future and I should advise you to communicate with them.

Yours sincerely,
Alec Jackson
Speedway Manager

Wally said: 'As a result of the letter I contacted West Ham who invited me to go with my bike to Rye House. They suggested that my old Douglas would be unsuitable but gave me a contact where I might be able to buy a speedway machine.

'The contact turned out to be Wal Phillips, the old Stamford Bridge and Wimbledon international, who took me to somewhere in Romford, or Ilford. The highlight of that visit was not handing over the £70 the Army gave me for my years fighting for King and country, but the thrill of seeing Roy Craighead and Bill Gilbert there tuning their machines. As a Wembley supporter, and to Wal Phillips's disgust, their autographs were more important than a rusty old pre-war speedway machine.

'I returned to my old local field and managed to do a few circuits before the residents threw me off. The following evening I gave the bike a quick burst along The Ridgeway in Mill Hill, but a near miss with a bus put a stop to that.

'There were lots of novices as well as me at Rye House the following Wednesday and they were all going round faster than me. But at the end of the day I was the only one to be offered a contract and put in a race at West Ham the following Tuesday.

'I fell off on the first bend. And I fell off again on the first bend the following week. A man named Frank Arnold came over to me and said: "I didn't believe you when you said you hadn't raced before. You are a bloody fool, you could have killed yourself out there tonight."

*Flying with the
Eagles at Eastbourne
– the 1947 Division
Three championship
winning side, from
left: Basil Harris,
Ron Clark, Wally,
Ken Tidbury (on
bike), Bob Sivyer,
Jock Grierson, Jimmy
Coy. In front Harry
Saunders.*

'It was arranged that I should go to Southampton on loan and I had one race to prove myself. I was more cautious that time and was leading my one race when my front tyre came off. After the meeting I approached the promoter to ask if he wanted to keep me, when he looked in his programme and saw I'd come last he said no.

'As I left, the promoter of the visiting team approached me and asked if I would ride for him. His name was Charlie Dugard who owned Eastbourne in the Third Division. I jumped at the chance and raced for them on Saturday afternoons because I was an instructor in the week at Hendon.

'I was reserve and Charlie was happy for me to miss the away matches. But Dennis Gray, who was probably the best of the Eastbourne riders, had a spill and injured his hand so I was put straight into the team. I raced for them for the rest of the season and became one of their top point scorers.'

Wally ended that season as the fifth highest scorer in the league behind such future big names as Cyril Roger, Basil Harris, Bob Oakley and Geoff Bennett.

He said: 'It soon became clear I could earn a lot more money as a speedway rider than a gas fitter, so I resigned the day job. I had to have transport so I bought a baker's van for £10. It was identical to Mr Jones's, the bumbling butcher in *Dad's Army*, even down to the oval windows beside the driver. The main problem was the gear lever, which had to be held in place so I had only one hand to steer the thing with, give hand signals and operate the hand brake because the footbrake didn't work. And some of the floor was missing.

'In 1948 the Eastbourne team moved to Hastings. During this season I was nominated to race against Bert Roger of Exeter for the Third Division Match Race Championship. I won at Hastings but broke a collarbone before the return match.

'Aub Lawson came to see me one day at Hastings and suggested I should return to West Ham. I agreed, and in my first meeting, which was at Wembley, I fell off on the first bend in both my reserve races. I wondered if the Big Stage was beyond me. Some years later I was knocked off at the same spot. The 'star' who knocked me off came and apologized because it wasn't me he was after, he said it was 'that b*****d Eric Williams.'

Wally's scores increased with the Hammers in the company of such top names as Eric Chitty *(See Page 133)*, Malcolm Craven, Cliff Watson and Lawson, and for a while the only rider to outscore him at the club was the then World Champion Jack Young *(See Page 143)*.

His career peak was probably the night of the 1950 World Final. His qualification was unremarkable. He squeezed into Wembley in thirteenth place on 29 points, the same number as one of the heroes of his youth, reigning World Champion Tommy Price.

It was a star-studded Final and included such high class performers as Vic Duggan, Jack Parker, Split Waterman, Aub Lawson, Ronnie Moore and Jack Young. But on the night Wally, described as the 'surprise runner-up', dropped points only to eventual title winner Fred Williams *(See Page 150)* and to the brilliant Graham Warren in his last ride, Heat 16.

Blond Bombshell Warren's name had been written on the trophy all season, he'd been that good, but in his crucial race with Williams he fell challenging for the lead to finish third. Williams confessed later that his tactics had been to frighten everyone of his

The magic moment: Just one point away from being World Champion, Wally is congratulated by Earl Mountbatten after his second place to Fred Williams in the 1950 World Final. Looking on from the left, Wembley boss Arthur Elvin, Speedway Control Board chairman R. Vernon C. Brook and Sunday Dispatch editor Charles Eade.

Traditional tractor ride for the 1950 Wembley top three. From the left Graham Warren, third, Wally and champion Fred Williams.

opponents by breaking the Wembley track record in the opening heat, which he did.

Wally's score of 13 put him in the unique position of being third in the old style World Championship averages table. Only Bluey Wilkinson and Ivan Mauger were above him because he appeared in just that one Final. His performance earned him eighth place in the First Division rankings, two below champion Williams four places above Duggan, and twelfth in the World Rankings.

Wally was extremely self-effacing because he was not always entirely convinced he was good enough to race in such exalted company. Chosen to ride for England in the third Test of 1952 series at Belle Vue, where he never scored well, he called the selectors and told them they had made a mistake. But gee-ed up by his mechanic who told him he never really tried at Belle Vue, he scored 11 points but was unable to prevent Australia winning 56 – 52.

Gee-ed up at Belle Vue: Lining up for the third Test in 1952, from left, Athur Forrest, Louis Lawson, Wally and Fred Williams.

Wally raced in many internationals, but almost certainly would have considered his real career peak the night he captained England in a Test match at West Ham. But, he said, his grandchildren would never believe him when he told them he was once captain of England – until I found a programme of the meeting and presented it to him so that he could prove it to them.

Soon afterwards I received a letter from Wal. It read:

And this is Wally in his England race jacket on his way to 11 points in the match.

I would like to thank you personally for giving me the 1954 programme of the Test Match against Australasia at West Ham when I was captain of England ...

Fortunately for England Arthur Forrest scored 15 points and Brian Crutcher was top scorer of the night with 17 points.

Thanks to Brian and Arthur I am able to tell my grandchildren I was captain of England on the night we beat Australasia 60 points to 48.

'Thanks for the memory, John.'

WALLY GREEN
(World No.2 1950)
Arkley, Hertfordshire

The West Ham international 'mafia': Cliff Watson, Wally, centre, and Jack Young.

Wally scored seven points. What he was far too modest to mention was that the match report said: *'Skipper Green opened magnificently with a tearaway win over his opposite number Jack Young.'*

Wally stayed at West Ham until retiring on medical advice in 1955, the year West Ham closed. He then started a successful business manufacturing cycle speedway bikes.

He was a lifelong enthusiastic member of the old Veteran Speedway Riders Association and regularly attended the *Vintage Speedway Magazine's* annual speedway birthday party at High Beech every February. He always wore his old West Ham team blazer which, even after he reached eighty, fitted him.

Wally died at the age of eighty-four, still owing Dicky Case £1.

Wally makes the maestro do the chasing at Belle Vue as he leads Jack Parker.

Mike Bast

A BLAST FROM THE PAST

STANDFIRST

One of America's least known but 'winningest' stars, Mike Bast, reveals why he decided it was not worth putting his life on the line or taking a chance on conquering Europe; how he rates his fellow Americans who did, such as triple World Champion Greg Hancock; why he regrets not going for the golden title himself; what he thinks of the Grand Prix system; what happened when speedway's irresistible force met speedway's immovable object' and why he wants to be remembered as a Bad Guy.

THE CITY OF Los Angeles is in an area prone to earthquakes. The magnitude of earthquakes is measured on the Richter Scale, with a value of between zero and eight. A really bad one is rated six.

The headline that blazed across the front page of the unique (and now tragically long-gone) Los Angeles-based *Speedway Magazine* for May 1984, as far as American fans were concerned, rated a perfect 10 on the Richter Scale. In other words: it was off the scale!

And in an area also not unfamiliar with the experience of mind-altering substances, it was literally mind-blowing – as if all the stars had suddenly fallen from the Star Spangled Banner.

Dominating: Mike Bast ahead of Gene Woods at Costa Mesa.

It contained only two words. Which by right should have been, in true tabloid tradition: SHOCK HORROR!

But the words that actually zapped the sport's faithful right between the eyes were: BAST QUITS!

It meant that the multi-titled, 16-year racing career of the least most internationally lauded of America's great track talents had hit the buffers. As a result of the irresistible speedway force meeting the immovable speedway object.

The irresistable speedway force being the forthright seven-times US National Champion Michael Joseph Bast, and the immovable speedway object being the irascible Czar of Costa Mesa and the Godfather of West Coast speedway, Harry Oxley.

The fall-out from the resultant conflagration was of megaton proportions. Sample quotes:

> *'If I've got to go out and put my life on the line to make*
> *Harry Oxley a good living, I don't need it.'* – Mike Bast.

> *'He's either lost his nerve, lost his desire to race, or something.'* – Harry Oxley.

> *'The joke is not Mike Bast, the joke is Harry Oxley.'* – Mike Bast.

> *'Whatever happens, Bast will complain.'* – Harry Oxley.

The blazing front page of Speedway Magazine *that carried the shock news to West coast speedway fans.*

All good, knockabout stuff. And there's more invective where that came from. But, don't go away, we'll come to that presently.

The name Mike Bast will not be readily familiar to many modern British or European enthusiasts, principally because his flirtation with European speedway was all too brief. And we will come to the reasons for that presently, as well.

Mike Bast is as underrated among the sport's major players as was the supremely skilled Egon Muller of Germany until, in 1983, Egon confounded the speedway world by sweeping to the World Championship title: 'Made us all look silly,' said Kenny Carter.

Yet each of them was, rightly, highly revered in his own land.

The Americans have a somewhat irritating phrase they use to describe success on the track – they say that a particular rider is the *'most winningest'*. And Mike Bast was certainly that. So much so that in one interview he found it necessary to deny that he was either 'a machine, a computer or a robot'.

His achievements on a speedway motorcycle, admittedly in California, must rank him alongside his inspirations, who were primarily the outstandingly talented fellow countrymen the Milne brothers, Jack and Cordy, and the stylishly brilliant Wilbur Lamoreaux (*See Page 83*), plus the latter day glamorous and charismatic Bruce Penhall.

No, I am not forgetting *Sudden* Sam Ermolenko, Greg Hancock or Billy *The Bullet* Hamill. Or that they are World Champions and that they all strutted their stuff in the grand arena. Or indeed the man who should have been America's seventh title holder but made it only to third place, Scott Autrey. Each paid their dues on the European scene, which Mike had his reasons for choosing not to do.

Below left: *Master of all he surveys … the czar of American speedway in all his exotic finery, Harry Oxley among the fans at his fabulous fiefdom, Costa Mesa.*

Below right: *Inspiration: The major modern influence, six times World Champion Ivan Mauger who changed Mike Bast's view of how speedway should be ridden.*

Mr Determined: Bast, the immovable 'I want to be the bad guy' object encountered by the Oxley irresistible force.

BAST MICHAEL JOSEPH: Born Van Nuys, California, January 6, 1953. First rode speedway at Whiteman Stadium in 1968. Rates his most memorable moment as winning the 1975 US title at the Los Angeles Coliseum. Went on to win seven national titles six California State Championships and uncountable main events at Costa Mesa and San *'The Only Reason For Wednesday Nghts'* Bernardino. The Bast record of seven US National titles has yet to be equalled.

Mike Bast's worst moment in speedway was seeing Geoff Curtis killed at the Sydney Showground in 1974. Speedway riders he admired include Barry Briggs, Ivan Mauger and Bruce Penhall. And the funniest thing he saw in speedway was watching Penhall ride naked at Bakersfield in 1976. He likes The Beatles and Willie Nelson and his hobbies are trail riding, guns and billiards. His other hobby, building houses, he turned into a full-time profession.

It is always as well to start things at the beginning. So before we get into the big Bast v Oxley Bust-Up, let's take a look at the Bast speedway origins.

JC: What was the attraction of speedway for you, and how did you first get into it?

MB: I had seen old pictures of Jack Milne racing speedway and it looked an interesting sport. Then in 1968 they staged an event in my home town of Pacoima, California. It was the first time it had been run there since the war. There were about four old Crockers and a couple of old JAPs, running around. The following week we took our Class-C flat track Bultacos out there. I was 15, my brother Steve was 16. In a couple of weeks there were a dozen or so proper speedway bikes, with 18 riders sharing bikes. And they got the show going.

JC: What ambitions did you have when you first started racing?

MB: My initial ambitions were to be like Kenny Roberts, to become a top Class-C flat track racer. Flat track racing was my serious goal and speedway was just a bit of fun. That all changed when I saw Ivan Mauger in 1969. He rode with Barry Briggs at my local track and it was unbelievable. That was how I wanted to ride, I wanted to be World Speedway Champion.

JC: I think your 'friend' Harry Oxley has said that few riders have had such an impact on US speedway as you (seven times US National Champion, six times California State Champion). That's putting you above lots of distinguished names. How do you feel about that?

MB: Grateful. That was nice of Harry to say it. I did what I had to do at the time.

JC: You didn't care for handicap racing – the 'big draw' in American speedway. Tell me about your row with Oxley that made you finally quit. And why you then came out of retirement to ride in the 1984 State Championship.

MB: Towards the end of my career, I was around 30 years old, all the top riders that I raced against, Penhall, Sigalos, Schwartz, the Morans, they had all gone to Europe. Harry filled the handicap program with Division 2 riders who kept falling down.

I told Harry that I only wanted to ride in the scratch races. Harry agreed, saying it would open up a slot for a youngster. I didn't ride handicap at all that season. I was riding only scratch races, five or six nights a week. The next season Harry told me that if I wanted to race at Orange County (Costa Mesa) I would have to ride handicaps too, not just scratch. So I rode round behind the rest, doing wheelies, to entertain the crowd.

After the second week of the season he suspended me, after making the deal the year before. I called the AMA, told them I was suspended. Their rules said the top 16 riders should take priority on the scratch program, but they did not support me. The other tracks still wanted me to race there, but I'd had enough. I preferred racing at San Bernardino. Costa Mesa was hard work, it was so small, but they had the biggest crowd, and paid the highest prize money. But I'd had enough, so I quit. My father-in-law helped me get into the construction business.

I was reigning State Champion in 1983, with a 15 point maximum. In 1984, although I had retired, John LaDouceur, the San Bernardino promoter, asked me to come back and defend my title. I agreed. I hadn't ridden all year. Mike Faria won it, I tied on points with Bobby Schwartz for second place, but Bobby won the run-off.

JC: The final rift with Harry Oxley over the handicaps was a bruising encounter. It all began, according to the report in *Speedway Magazine* at the time, with a letter Harry sent to all 40yd and 50yd Division 1 riders warning them that if they didn't transfer for three weeks in a row they would be left off the programme.

It caused such outrage that Harry felt compelled to send a letter of apology which contained the phrase 'with the exception of one man'. He then mailed a note to Mike Bast saying:

'You will realise that you are who I was referring to. Since you have chosen to make a fool of yourself and a mockery of handicap racing at Costa mesa, I have no alternative other than to leave you off the program starting this Friday night. I think the time has come that you re-assess your career as a speedway rider.'

Bast retorted: 'I've promoted the sport more than anyone for 16 years, won more races and more titles than all of them put together and done more for the sport than anyone else. I could name you 12 guys that if they'd come back to America from Britain there'd be 12 guys off the handicap at Costa Mesa because they are not good enough.

'Harry's putting guys in there who ride like my son, who is five years old, and expects them to race against guys like me who are built to show. I'm not going to put my life on the line to compete against people like he's got out there. Harry's got to be smarter than that.'

It would take a miracle, said Bast, for him to reconsider his decision to retire. No miracle was forthcoming…

JC: When it came down to it, you had won so many US titles yet had only a brief time in Europe. Did you not want to widen your speedway horizon?

MB: After meeting Ivan I seriously wanted to be World Champion, but in those days, American speedway was a lucrative business. I was doing very well winning National Championships, State Championships and track championships. I owned a home, and I worked as a stunt man in the movie business during the off-season. When I got married in 1974 I was making $60,000 or $70,000 a year in America. I started working in the construction business with my father-in-law, I wanted to start a family, I had a lot going on here. The British League offered a couple of pounds a point, there really wasn't the incentive.

JC: I believe you did have a temporary flirtation with British speedway. I know Steve rode for Wembley briefly. Why did you not persevere as others did?

MB: Steve rode for Wembley for a while in 1970. But he got homesick and he came home and got married and settled back here. Kings Lynn and Belle Vue wanted me to ride for them. Ivan and Barry Briggs both offered to help, but there was no compelling reason to go. The money really did not make it worthwhile.

The ill-fated trip to England in 1977: Mike (left) and Bruce Penhall confer at the Intercontinental Final of the World Championship. Things were not made easy for them and they felt 'everyone was against us'.

Taking on the World. Mike Bast leads Malcolm Simmons and Rick Woods in one of the international World Series hosted by the Americans.

JC: You and Penhall qualified to ride in the 1977 Intercontinental Final of the World Championship in London. How were you treated in Britain? I understand you were not given good practice facilities. And what were the practical arrangements for getting bikes to Britain and what pit crew back-up did you have?

MB: Bruce and I beat Scott Autrey at Orange County, and qualified for the two slots in the Intercontinental Final. We went over to England and hoped to ride in some British League meetings to get some familiarity with the tracks. But between the AMA and the FIM they could not arrange for us to compete in any races before the Continental Final, not even in the second half events. The result was we finished up 14th and 16th in the Intercontinental Final.

Showing them how at San Bernardino where Mike preferred racing because 'Costa Mesa was hard work, it was too small'.

We took our own bikes over. The late George Wenn was an Englishman living in California and was the top engine tuner. He came along as my mechanic and built the bikes up there and showed us around the place. Generally, we did not get much co-operation over there. Everyone was against us. They all thought Scott Autrey should have been in the meeting. But the qualifier was on the little track at Orange County, Bruce and I raced there every week. Scott had been racing on quarter mile tracks and couldn't compete with us. In reality, they were right. He should have been given a place in the event instead, he could have won the world title.

I regret not going for the World Championship, because I know I could have won it. I raced against Ivan, Ole Olsen and Anders Michanek and beat them all at Orange County. They all tried to persuade me to go to Europe. Bruce put in the time, the money and the effort and won two World Championships for his efforts.

JC: You travelled the States promoting the sport, and were critical of Penhall because he didn't.

MB: I would not say I was critical of Bruce. He and I rode together in Southern California, but he decided to go to Europe to go for the World Championship. I wanted to try and help the sport grow here, by travelling around running schools.

JC: What were the cash rewards of racing when you were riding? Were you a full-time professional racer?

MB: My average was around $40,000. Harry used to pay us 30 per cent of the gate and there were crowds of 10,000 people every Friday night at Orange County. It peaked around 1978, when Bruce and Dennis left. You could make $1,000 for a main event win in those days. I frequently made $1,200 or $1,300 a night in prize money.

JC: You said that when you quit you wanted to promote – yet at the time US speedway was at its height after Penhall's two world title wins – and you were predicting that the sport in the US was doomed. Your prediction seems to have come true.

MB: When I quit racing speedway, I wanted to promote. I looked around in Pico Rivera, the San Fernando Valley and Devonshire Downs. But it was hard working with city councils and the fairgrounds boards. I even looked in Stockton in Northern California. I had no trade, all I had done was ride speedway for all those years, but I understood it well from the riders' side.

Harry kept the sport local, but I wanted to take it nationwide. I soon learned that promoting involves more than just preparing the track. I lacked sales skills, I needed financial backing, riders, bikes, etc. I was in over my head. The sport really hasn't come back since that time. It has gone from six nights a week to one.

JC: You felt that some of your contemporaries preferred 'the good life' instead of being as dedicated to the sport as you were, and you seemed to resent this.

MB: Absolutely. With the exception of Bruce Penhall and Dennis Sigalos, they all wanted to go and party! I always got mad at those guys. They showed up with dirty bikes and dirty leathers. But overall Americans have nothing lacking when it comes to talent.

JC: Oxley said that you 'went on strike' because he wouldn't pay you $50 appearance money – yet he also says you were getting $500 a night. How many nights a week were you riding?

MB: No, I didn't go on strike. Harry's got it mixed up. I said I wanted $100 appearance money, for each time I won the National Championship. I got to about five and he cut me off. At one time I was getting $500 a night appearance money at each of five tracks every week. Harry put up a sign posting a reward one time to try and get people to beat me.

JC: Oxley also said that technically you are the best rider the US has ever had – do you agree?

MB: I can't blow my own horn, but I guess if you count up National Championships I suppose I was. My brother was a talented rider, I always thought he was much better than me, but he quit too easily. Ole Olsen was a very talented rider, but Ivan always impressed me the most, he rode with his head. He followed me round for four laps once and came by on the inside on the last lap. He told me I left a big gap there, I guess I must have done.

JC: What is your real opinion of all the guys who did fly the coop – Autrey, Penhall, Sigalos, Schwartz, Ermolenko, the Morans, Hancock, Hamill?

MB: I admired them all for going and broadening their horizons. Sometimes I regret staying and riding round Orange County every week. I think Greg winning his third World Championship in 2014 is fantastic. As you know I have watched Greg since he was a junior rider in southern California. I have followed him all through his career and he has always been nothing but professional, an outstanding role model for the up and coming young riders as well as a superb representative for USA speedway. I am proud of his accomplishments and proud to call him a friend.

Helping the sport to grow by passing on the knowledge: Mike with a trainee at one of his speedway schools.

JC: What was the highest point of your career? What gave you the biggest sense of achievement, or what moment will you always remember?

MB: A tough one, but I think it was winning the US Championship at the Los Angeles Coliseum in 1975. I had already won it twice, my brother Steve had won it twice, Rick Woods had won it twice. That was a fun night. I was the first guy to win it three times. After that the other National Championships were much easier. And 1975 was the only year the championship was not held at Costa Mesa. Harry and Jack Milne and Barry Briggs wanted to hold the event on a neutral ground, maybe they wanted to give everyone a chance to beat me!

JC: And the lowest?

MB: No question about it, when Harry said I was banned from racing for not riding handicap races. Can you imagine, he told me I couldn't ride and I had won more championships than anybody? I tried to talk to him about it, but he said I was making a mockery of the sport. That was a low. Had it not been for that, I would have continued riding. Maybe he did me a favour. It enabled me to get on and concentrate on my real estate business.

JC: Have you ever thought of making a comeback?

MB: Never. I quit while I was ahead.

JC: What have you been doing since you left the track?

Speedway USA, from left: Mike Bast, Alan Christian, Bruce Penhall, Mike Curoso, Steve Bast, Ron Preston, Mike Faria.

MB: I got my licence as a general contractor in 1984. I didn't waste any time. Before that I worked for my father-in-law in the winter, and quitting speedway enabled me to work at it full time. Since then I have accumulated houses, which continue to pay dividends.

JC: What do you think of the sport now?

MB: I still love it. Speedway to me will always be the best sport there is. Dick Mann, a mile track racer, said to me: 'You know you speedway guys are lucky, you only have to go 45 miles per hour.' I told him: 'You are wrong, it's tough. You guys on the mile track have a long rest down the straightaway, but the speedway rider has a continuous minute of hard work.'

Speedway is the greatest most spectacular motorcycle sport in the world. I try to get down to Auburn every Friday night that I can to watch my cousin Bart.

JC: What do you think of the Grand Prix format, as opposed to the 16-rider 20-heat championship format?

MB: Its fabulous. One night was tough. The GP format gives a rider more chance to think what he is doing. Every sport in the world is done on a points system over many, many meetings.

The hardest thing to do is what Ivan did, winning the one-off World Championship six times. Anything can go wrong, break a chain, get a flat tyre, maybe feel sick that day. The format now with the points accumulation makes much more sense. If I were 20 I would be over there myself! The one night thing gives you no margin for error, like when Bruce and I went over in 1977. I look back at my National Championship wins and I don't know how I did it!

JC: How should US speedway go about trying to bring more kids into the sport?

MB: More schools, more tracks, more incentives. It needs to be exposed in new places.

Peerless and multi-titled: Mike on the rostrum after winning his fourth national championship in 1976.

JC: Have you ever tried any other forms of motorcycle sport?

MB: I still race vintage motocross, several times a year. I go to Colorado, Oregon, Washington and Arizona to race in the American Historic Motorcycle Racing Association series. I have 15 bikes in my garage. I have never tried road racing. I have trophies for riding trials. Its good for balance, timing and throttle control.

JC: How would you like to be remembered?

MB: As a villain, just like I was once, but also as the best ever. I had the villain image. The promoters didn't like me. I won too many races so the other riders didn't like me. Sometimes even the crowd didn't like me. I should have worn 'Bad Guy' black leathers, not white.

But I did get on well with Ivan Mauger, Anders Michanek, and Ole Olsen and the guys who came over here from Europe. They knew I was a good man.

Overall, I consider myself both lucky and successful. I love my wife and my kids. We enjoy life.

I can thank speedway for teaching me how to be there, to arrive prepared, and to strive to win. I learned how to experience success and carried it through to my business and to the rest of my life.

John Chaplin would like to gratefully acknowledge the assistance of Gary Roberts in the preparation of this interview. The questions were sent to him in California and he did the legwork by going to see Mike Bast, recording his answers and adding a few vital contributions of his own. Sadly, early in 2015, Mike Bast suffered a stroke. His recovery at home in California will take some months. A fund has been started to help with his medical bills, which are expected to be in the region of $50,000.

Oliver Hart

THRILL-A-MINUTE WITH LAUGHING BOY

SOON AFTER THE TAPES went up on Heat 6 at Owlerton Stadium, Sheffield on 24 July sixty three years ago, much of the compelling magic spectacle of speedway racing was lost forever.

Lined up for that fateful race were young First Division Odsal wizzkid Arthur Forrest and high flying Second Division Motherwell star Derek Close, alongside veterans Wilf Jay of Second Division Glasgow Ashfield, and Forrest's team mate at Bradford, Oliver Hart.

The reason for mixing the talent from the divisions was because it was a special invitational meeting staged by Oliver Hart's Belle Vue mentor and former fiery England international Frank Varey. Frank, pre-war Ace known as El Diablo Rojo (The Red Devil), was promoting open events at Sheffield, a track affected badly by the iniquitous government entertainment tax and at the time without a regular league licence.

The highly popular Oliver Hart was one of the sport's most colourful characters and referred to by the speedway journalists – who loved to hang imaginative labels on the stars of the day – as Mr Entertainment, and the Greatest Showman Of Them All. The great Basil Storey, Editor of the highly influential *Speedway Gazette,* described Oliver as 'the guy with a perpetual big grin', and so he called Oliver Laughing Boy.

To the terrace fans, friend and foe alike, he was affectionately known as just plain Olly.

Many characters in the cinders game have down the years laid claim to – or had thrust upon them – the title of Mr Entertainment and the Greatest Showman Of Them All: Roarin' Johnnie Hoskins himself, for a start, Lloyd 'Sprouts' Elder for another, and also the daredevil pre-war speedway rider/stuntman Putt Mossman.

Fittingly the accolade sat well with the spectacular style of Oliver Hart. But it all came literally to a spectacular crashing and tragic end in Heat 6 that July day at Owlerton.

Derek Close recalled: 'Yes, I do indeed remember what happened. There was Wilf Jay, Arthur Forrest , Olly and myself in the race. Arthur Forrest and Olly made the gate in front of us, I was lying third and Wilf Jay was fourth. Sheffield is a beautiful track, lovely surface, and you just wound it on, held the throttle wide open and kept going.

'When I first started riding the tracks were deep cinders and of course later on it gradually got to be shale. Olly was a leg-trailer, one of the most spectacular riders I have ever seen. He was in front with Arthur Forrest right behind, and unfortunately, it being a slick track, Olly just dropped his bike. All I could do was throw my bike down. But when Olly came down on the track I just slid into him. It was very tragic really, I couldn't do anything about it.'

Reports say that another rider hit him as well.

Derek said: 'That might be so, and that other rider would have been Arthur Forrest. I'm afraid I don't know whether Arthur hit Olly – he might have done. He was on the inside. I know that Wilf Jay was behind me, but on the outside and he got his bike down as well. Olly was hurt very badly, it was one of my big regrets of speedway and I've often wondered whether I could have done anything else.

'Someone showed me a sequence of photographs of what happened, one after the other, and I don't think I could have done anything more … it would have been impossible. It

The perpetual grin was there right at the beginning as a member of the 1936 New Brighton side. Oliver is second from the right. Brother Ron is kneeling at the front on the right and Ernie Price, later a team mate at Bradford is second from left.

*Happy-go-lucky
Olly in the Belle Vue
pits demonstrating
why they called him
Laughing Boy.*

was a very sad thing. Olly rode pre-war and I always admired how he used to ride. He was the most spectacular rider. He was wonderful to watch and it was a tragic thing in my life when that happened. But of course it happens in just a fraction of a second. The track was that slick, and that's why Olly dropped his bike in the first place.

'Frank Varey looked after the track and I always enjoyed riding there. It was a great track, beautiful to ride and one of my favourites. But it was very unfortunate what happened to Oliver there.'

After the accident Olly was taken to Sheffield Infirmary. He had a broken back, collarbone and five broken ribs and severe concussion. The doctors did not expect him to live and he was on the critical list for several days. Even then it was doubtful he would ever walk again.

But he was on his feet within four weeks, the Odsal crowd greeting him ecstatically when he went on to the centre green and told them he would ride again … on special occasions.

In all the 19 years of his speedway career Oliver was never going to be World Champion, though he did reach international and world class. Because of his unique ability, the crowds never knew what it would be when Olly was on the track – the thrill-a-minute Laughing Boy from Lancashire.

Oliver Hart's racing career came to an abrupt end in that crash at Sheffield, but ever since it began at New Brighton in 1935 he was truly one of the greatest speedway stylists and a maestro of the lost art of broadsiding.

In a priceless little paperback booklet, *Broadside To Fame: The Drama Of The Speedways*, published on the crest of the biggest boom the sport has ever known just before the 1947 season, its author Leonard Sandys, of *The Sporting Life* newspaper, described Olly thus: 'Oliver Hart – the merry madcap who is perhaps the biggest thriller on the speedways. You wouldn't call him a champion, but Olly remains the irrepressible joker who roars into bends with a wide open throttle and a who-cares-a-damn leg-trail style. As always, he remains the firm favourite of thousands, a happy-go-lucky artist who guarantees any crowd value for money.'

Well, you can't say fairer than that. And two words stand out which sum up Olly's speedway philosophy: 'favourite' and 'artist'. Whether he was riding for your team or for the opposition, you knew you were in for a spectacular demonstration of pure artistry when Olly paraded his skills. With his never-give-up style, no true speedway fan could help but consider him to be a universal favourite.

It was an era when there was still an abundance of trailers among the big names who had been the great pre-war pioneers. Among them men such as Wally Lloyd, and Walter Hull at Belle Vue, Bert Spencer and Ted Bravery at Norwich, Roy Dook and Bob Lovell at Birmingham, Geoff Pymar and Mick Mitchell at New Cross, Max Grosskreutz at Bradford, Colin Watson and Bob Harrison at West Ham, Lloyd 'Cowboy' Goffe at Wimbledon, Fred 'Kid' Curtis at Middlesbrough, Doug McLachlan at Newcastle and Len Williams at Sheffield.

But Olly had something extra – his terrific personality. In his unique publication, *The Romance Of The Speedway*, which appeared around 1930, Sprouts Elder remarks in his chapter entitled *The Man And The Machine:* 'Dirt-track racing is no carnival … it's a serious business.' Oliver Hart, would have disagreed.

Though approaching the sport with a degree of responsible seriousness that is only right and proper, bearing in mind it is a dangerous occupation, every time he went out to ride it was carnival time. And the fans loved every magic moment.

There were three speedway Hart brothers. Oliver, Stanley, who was killed racing at Birmingham in 1937, and Ron. They had every advantage. Their father, also Oliver, was a successful businessman who had started out with a humble horse and cart hauling cotton and coal. He graduated into transport and a farm with a sizeable land acreage.

Oliver senior did not approve of his sons' interest in motorcycling and, to discourage them, took them to a hospital to see some young men who had been severely injured riding bikes.

It didn't work. The boys were soon refining their technique on 22 acres of their father's farmland. Eventually Oliver landed a trial at Belle Vue.

And this is the real story of how be became speedway's most celebrated leg-trailer. He began as a foot-forward rider but at the Belle Vue trial he fell awkwardly onto his left knee. At first he feared his track career was over, but he went back to Belle Vue even though the knee had not healed properly.

A recent biography reveals: 'The knee was not ready for the pressure and Oliver allowed his leg to trail. It is not true that Oliver had no choice but to leg-trail because of the accident to his knee. He lost no mobility and could walk and run without difficulty. The choice of style was his. He remained competitive to the end of his career.'

Until the war, Oliver rode mainly in the Second Division for Liverpool – it didn't do him and his brother any harm either that his father was chairman of the Liverpool management company - Edinburgh, and later Belle Vue.

When Stanley was killed, Oliver and Ron quit speedway. But in the booklet *The Harts Of Coppull*, an account of the family's business and sporting activities, it is said: 'Over the winter of 1937/38 Stanley must have contacted Oliver because he reappeared at Belle Vue.'

Was there some sort of divine intervention? The biographer says it was written 'tongue in cheek, but no one in the family really knew'.

During the war the Hart farming enterprise apparently meant that Oliver was in a reserved occupation, and it enabled him to join the select band of riders who kept speedway alive at the old Hyde Road track in Manchester during hostilities.

Olly suddenly found himself banging elbows with the really big names in the sport, high-ranking world class talent of the calibre of the Parker brothers, Jack and Norman, and Alec Statham from Harringay *(See Page 112)*, Belle Vue experts Frank Varey, Bill Kitchen *(See Page 56)* and Eric Langton *(See Page 33)*, Ron Johnson *(See Page 39)* and Bill Longley from New Cross, Eric Chitty from West Ham *(See Page 133)*, the future World Champion Tommy Price of Wembley *(See Page 90)* and the man soon to be Oliver's skipper at Odsal/Bradford, the rapidly emerging Ron Clarke *(See Page 127)*.

When the list of award winners came to be published, Oliver's name was on the 1941 Northern Championship and the 1942 Track championship. There were also the 1941 pairs events, the Speedway Cup and National Trophy, both with Bill Kitchen. And they went on to tie for the 1941 British Empire Best Pairs with Eric Langton and Frank Varey, win the All England Best Pairs in 1942 and the British Empire title again in 1943. In 1944 Oliver won the Speedway Cup once more, this time with Harringay's Les Wotton.

Laughing Boy had come of speedway age, and just after the end of the war he took part in the ENSA track tour of Europe entertaining the occupying troops.

Prior to the 1946 season the available riders were pooled with the idea of an even and fair spread of talent, and the lad from the North found himself in the great southern metropolis in the colours of Wimbledon, number two to Dons captain Norman Parker. As well as being pooled, riders were graded for pay purposes, and Oliver was in Grade 2. It is interesting to note that the rating gave him 25shillings (£1.25p) a start and 25 shillings a point.

Even more interesting – or, compared with today's financial rewards, maybe astounding would be a more appropriate word – a rider who risked all and ended a 14-heat, four ride league match with maximum points would earn himself a grand total of £20 for his night's

SPEEDWAY'S LAUGHING BOY

Apart from his success during the wartime meetings in Manchester, Oliver was a member of the ENSA team which entertained the troops in Occupied Europe and won the Brussells Challenge Trophy in early 1947.

Oliver the fully-fledged star in a thrilling duel with Fred Williams at Wembley.

work. This during a period when ten million *(that's right, 10,000,000)* people paid to see daredevils like Oliver risk life and limb.

The tight Wimbledon circuit at Plough Lane was not the most ideal canvas for a leg-trailer such as Oliver to demonstrate his skills, but in that first post-war season in the top flight he was second only to Parker in the score chart, though the Dons finished fourth out of the six teams in the senior division.

The highly regarded and experienced speedway journalist Tom Morgan – *Broadsider* of *The People* newspaper – made this comment when summing up outstanding 1946 performances: 'A name I would like to put high on my list is Oliver Hart. Now Oliver … is a godsend to every promoter in that he always gives a spectacular show. If only for that Oliver has probably pulled in as many people through the gates as the top ranking stars.

'Hart rides out into the great wide open spaces, keeping everything turned on around the bends, literally rounding them on his ear, giving the crowd full value for their money but at the same time making himself the despair of his partners who have ideas of team riding. Oliver scorns team riding. All he wants to do is get out there and have a bash. And bash he does. The crowd love him for it. What's more, Oliver loves every minute of it.'

Even so, Hart's heart was really in the North, where his business interests were, and Oliver figured in a three-way winter transfer that took Bill Longley from Odsal back to his spiritual home at New Cross, Les Wotton from New Cross to take Oliver's place at Wimbledon and Oliver to Odsal. And there he stayed. Everyone was happy, especially Oliver who was more at home on the near 400 yard Bradford track than the 343 yards of Wimbledon.

And Olly's star went on rising. He prefaced the 1948 season by representing England in the winter Test series which put him in 11th place in the Australian rankings, one above 1937 World Champion Jack Milne. It was the first time he had made it into the international arena – though his cheeky face can be seen peering behind his peers at the first post-war Test in England at Bradford, his home track, in 1947.

The 1948 domestic season was when it all really happened for Olly. He topped the Bradford score chart and finally reached the substitue World Final at Wembley, the Speedway Riders Championship Final, injury keeping him out of the previous season's big occasion. On a night when Prince Philip presented the top prize to winner Vic Duggan, Oliver finished equal sixth with Jack Parker in the star-studded field which included Ron Johnson, Wilbur Lamoreaux, Malcolm Craven, Bill Gilbert, Split Waterman and Eric Chitty.

The season earned Oliver 9th place in the World Rankings above Eric Chitty, Graham Warren, Split Waterman and Tommy Price.

Of course, the speedway times they were a-changing. Riders who put their foot forward were beginning to get to the chequered flags first far more often, and leg-trailing was falling out of fashion. So were cinder tracks, whose deep racing surfaces provided nice convenient cushions for holding up the spectacular likes of Oliver Hart, and shale was taking over. But Oliver never changed his style.

The reason was revealed by Olly's old Bradford boss John S. Hoskins, after a party at the Harts' to celebrate the twenty-first birthday of Oliver's son. The conversation, according to Honest John, went like this: 'What did you do on *your* twenty-first, Oliver?'

Oliver: 'My old dad bought me a speedway machine.'

Hoskins: 'A JAP?'

Oliver: 'Oh, yes. I took it to Belle Vue for practise, fell off a dozen times and finally broke my kneecap. Still got the scars, you see, and that broken knee made me a leg-trailer. I would never put my leg forward.'

Hoskins: 'I never heard that before.'

Oliver: 'No one ever asked me.'

Not many people know this, but after the crash that ended Oliver's racing career, his ability at shooting almost got him into Britain's Olympic team. But at trials in Spain he objected to be expected to fire at live targets and he quit on principal ... and no doubt disgust.

His love of speedway remained. After Odsal closed in 1956, he and his old Boomerangs captain Ron Clarke reopened the track briefly the following year. Oliver was back on the track ... driving the grader. And he built a 200 yard training circuit on the farm where newcomers could rent bikes.

According the *The Harts Of Coppull* account, Oliver's final ride on a speedway bike was in the celebration of 60 years of speedway at Hackney in 1968 in the Old Timers' Race. Half way down the back straight his chain came off and Oliver parked the machine on the centre green, visibly annoyed ... a showman to the end.

The end for Oliver came in 1983. He was cremated in Wigan and his ashes scattered in the St John's garden of remembrance at Coppull, the church his father had carried stone to with his horse and cart during its construction.

There has never been another even remotely like Oliver Hart.

For old time's sake ... and the fun of it. Old veterans Oliver and mentor Frank (El Diablo Rojo) Varey put on their old Aces race jackets at the old Belle Vue.

THE HART CRASH REPORTS

The meeting was a challenge match between Sheffield and Odsal and the *Speedway Star* of 2 August 1952 reported:

'Oliver Hart, Odsal, fractured his spine and suffered head and shoulder injuries. He was leading in Heat 6 when he crashed heavily. His team mate, Arthur Forrest and Derek Close, the Motherwell rider guesting for Sheffield, who were close behind were unable to avoid a collision and they too crashed heavily. Luckily Forrest and Close escaped with a shaking. Hart was removed to Sheffield Infirmary.'

Scores: *Sheffield 37: Close 10, Semmens, Robinson 6, Hewett 5, G. Newton, Jay 4, Mason, Cooper 1.*
Odsal 47: Forrest 11, Rigg 9, D. Oliver, Crossland 7, Wright 6, Hart, R. Clarke 3, Hughes 1

Speedway Gazette did not carry a report of the meeting, probably because it was not an official fixture, but printed a news item which said that Oliver's captain Ron Clarke talked his way into the ward at midnight and stayed for four hours during which time the pair of them discussed their mutual business interests, ending with a request by Oliver to be taken to Sheffield on a stretcher to present a trophy.

Speedway News also did not carry a match report, but a news item informed readers:

'Oliver Hart, greatest exponent of the leg-trailing style, seriously injured in a crash at Sheffield last Thursday, and his twin brother Ron Hart, have both retired from speedway. In the fall when he (Oliver) was hit by two riders, he sustained a broken back, five fractured ribs and a broken collarbone. At Sheffield Infirmary he was said to be comfortable.'

In the same issue *Speedway News* Editor Sammy Samuel, under the headline 'SPORT'S BLACKEST MONTH', said he had also to report the death of Norah Booth, the Odsal secretary and joint promoter with her husband Bruce Booth at Halifax, who had been killed in a car crash, and that Wimbledon's American star Ernie Roccio had been killed in a racing crash at West Ham.

A

B

C

D

E

The John Somerville Collection

A: *Moments from disaster: Wilf Jay, Arthur Forrest and Derek Close bear down on Oliver Hart who is out of the picture.*
B: *All four riders are down. Forrest is far left, with Close, Jay and Oliver all tangled up on the right by the fence.*
C: *Ambulance men go to the aid of the riders. Jay and Close are sitting up but Oliver is obviously badly hurt.*
D: *More help is on the way and Close starts to try and go to the aid of the stricken Oliver.*
E: *Close is up on his feet as the ambulance men reach Oliver. Jay, still down, surveys the crash scene.*

Eric Langton
'THE GREATEST OF THEM ALL...'

ANYTHING TO DO WITH bikes interested the Langton brothers, Eric and Oliver. Long before speedway racing was introduced to England, the name of Langton was well known in connection with motorcycling sports of every description.

The pair were fascinated spectators at the first meeting in the north at Audenshaw, now hemmed in by the spider's web of Greater Manchester's modern motorway system, and not a million miles away from the Hyde Road site that was to become the world's most famous and finest speedway track.

What the Langtons witnessed that early March day in 1928 gave them the notion that dirt-track racing was a glorious opportunity to widen their horizons and add considerably to their worldly wealth.

Eric recalled: 'In 1928 a speedway rider could earn approximately £20 a week (£660 or £34,320 a year in today's money), which was about the same as the Prime Minister was paid at the time. A Member of Parliament earned £400 a year (£13,200 now), and a 20-year-old apprentice toolmaker was paid less than 30 shillings (£1.50 – that's £49.50 a week or £2,574 a year now) for a 47-plus hour week.'

The Langtons wasted no time. When a meeting was staged at the Blackpool trotting track the following month the brothers were there, and reports described them as 'outstanding performers', along with another young man destined for international fame and fortune, Harry Riley Lees, more affectionately later known as Ginger to his hordes of admirers at Wembley.

An early accident hindered the progress of Oliver, and it was Eric, with his brother's mechanical backing, who went on to reach the very top in the new sport. Eric Kemp Langton, born in Leeds in 1907, soon began to demonstrate that, up north, of all the English riders, he was the one who was going to cause the Australian expert pioneers the most concern.

In 1929, when league racing rescued speedway racing from a swift and ignominious extinction as a common circus freakshow, Eric captained the Leeds team to the first northern Dirt Track League Championship. In doing so he caught the attention of Eric E.O. Spence the astute Belle Vue boss who was in the process of putting together the team of invincibles that was to make the Aces the world's finest in the mid-Thirties.

E.O. stood no nonsense. Cabled from Argentina one winter by some of his riders who were down on their luck and wanted him to send them their boat fares home, he sent a one-word cable in return: 'Swim!'

Langton's outstanding ability, which saw him described as having the 'devastating habit of being able to win whenever he feels it necessary', created a legend around him. It was that 'Langton is Belle Vue, and Belle Vue is Langton.' Of which more later.

Yet his cinders career very nearly never reached the starting tapes. In 1926, riding back to Leeds from a Bradford and Leeds Motor Club meeting he was knocked from his machine. It was, said Eric, a terrible accident – a broken thigh and jaw and a crushed skull. It was so terrible, explained Eric, 'I was thought to be dead. I was taken to the hospital morgue where I stayed until the next day when it was discovered that I was breathing and I was revived.'

Young and adventurous, at the end of the 1929 British season the Langtons, along with such major stars as Lloyd 'Sprouts' Elder, Buzz Hibberd, Bob Harrison, Herbert 'Dusty' Haigh, brother Oliver and Max Grosskreutz, joined the A.J. Hunting speedway circus which toured the Argentine where Eric's long time Belle Vue team partner Frank Varey's

Causing the Australian experts concern: Eric, wearing his England captain's star, and rival skipper Vic Huxley before the fourth Test in 1931. It was a triumph for Eric, he led England to a 53 – 41 win.

Left: *Clash of the giants: Eric lines up alongside reigning British Champion Tom Farmndon before a match race at Belle Vue in 1934. Eric had held the title briefly the previous season.*

Right: *A cinder-stained family gathering in the Manchester pits. Eric is on the far right with Bill Kitchen next to him and brother Oliver next. Bill's father is in the dark suit and Eric's father is on the far left.*

crimson riding sweater earned him the famous title El Diablo Rojo (The Red Devil).

Eric said: 'There I competed with some of the world's best riders and by the end of that South American season I was able to beat them. I returned to England for the 1930 season and found that somehow I had signed to ride for Belle Vue for ever. As a result I rode for Belle Vue for the whole of my career.'

But Langton was always his own man. At the end of the 1932 season British Champion Jack Parker broke a collar bone which prevented him defending his title against Eric, who was the champion at the start of the 1933 season.

Of course the time came for him to meet his first challenger, who happened to be Ron Johnson of Crystal Palace, a Saturday track, the same race night as Belle Vue's. The competition then was a home and away match race series with a decider on a neutral track if necessary.

Eric told the Control Board that he would defend his title, but only at Belle Vue. Going to Crystal Palace would have meant him deserting the Aces on a Saturday night – something he was not prepared to do. The Control Board reminded him of the rules, but Eric would have none of it, so they took away his title.

Eric offered the fans no explanation for his action. *Speedway News* magazine pointed out: 'Had Langton ridden the match at the Palace tomorrow (Saturday) he would have missed Belle Vue's home fixture with Plymouth.' Eric's integrity was such, it seemed, that he placed the fortunes of his team even above personal glory.

Then, in the first Test against Australia at Wembley Eric, having reeled off four straight wins for England, got what our television commentator friends now call 'all out of shape' and rode over the grass. Though it gained him no advantage, he was disqualified. Petulantly he declined to take his final ride and was promptly disciplined by not being chosen for any more Tests that year.

Another display of 'personality' came in 1946 when league racing resumed after the war. An agreed pooling system of available talent was organised, but Eric's name was not listed.

Teamwork: Eric (outside) and Jack Parker – great rivals and great friends – combine to outride Australia's Lionel Van Praag (outside) and Vic Huxley in the second Test at New Cross in 1935.

Then, after all teams had been allocated, Eric decided to ride – but only for the Aces. After all, he had signed to race 'for Belle Vue for ever'. Which threw the speedway world into turmoil.

Rival promotions complained that Belle Vue would be too strong with Eric in the side. Again he wouldn't budge and he rode for the Aces in 1946 and 1947. By a twist of speedway fate, Eric's old rival Parker had been appointed the Belle Vue captain and an uneasy, but respectful, truce was established between the pair of them. Today they would be considered megastars.

It was as a team man that Eric excelled, and in the Thirties he led a Belle Vue side that was excellent all through and dominated between 1933 and 1936. The Aces included Bill Kitchen, Frank Charles *(See Page 44)*, Joe Abbott, Max Grosskreutz, Walter Hull, Bob Harrison, Dusty Haigh and Frank 'El Diablo Rojo' Varey, whose partnership with Eric became the scourge of speedway.

Eric described to me the understanding they had. 'Frank's style of riding wide suited my white line method. I always tried to get into the first corner in the lead and then wait for Frank to appear on my outside. From then on I filled the vulnerable gap inside him and geared my speed to his. If he didn't make the first corner I tried to slow the race so that he could catch up.'

It is called team riding – and is virtually a lost art among modern riders.

Eric's 29th birthday was on 10 September, 1936. It was also the birthday of what has been described as 'the greatest event ever organised in speedway history' – the first official World Championship Final at the Empire Stadium Wembley.

High drama at the first official World Championship final at Wembley in 1936. Eric displays mixed emotions watching Lionel Van Praag presented with the championship trophy after their decider by world land and water speed ace Sir Malcolm Campbell.

The meeting reached its climax at around 10.30 pm. The authorities had been afraid that not many people would turn up, but 66,018 did and their total attention was focussed on the two men crouching over their machines before the trembling tapes at the Wembley starting gate – Eric Kemp Langton of England and Belle Vue, Lionel Van Praag of Australia and Wembley.

It couldn't have been scripted better; a dramatic run-off for the title between Langton, the favourite to win and Van Praag, the Wembley team captain and local hero.

In only a few seconds one of them would be forever immortalised by claiming the title no man had ever held officially before, Speedway Champion Of The World. There was tension down on the track and off the track too. It rippled round the soaring cliffs of the packed Empire Stadium terraces.

Suddenly, as the two motors roared to full revs, the atmosphere of incredible expectancy was shattered by Langton. His machine nudged the tapes … and they broke.

PANDEMONIUM!

The biggest meeting, certainly in the brief eight-year history of the sport, was plunged from the heights of an incredibly dramatic deciding climax, to the depths of anti-climax. But, instead of being excluded as the speedway rules dictated he should have been, Langton lined up once more with Van Praag for the most important four laps of their careers.

What the huge crowd did not know, and was not to be revealed for almost half a century, was that an agreement had been struck by the two men out there in the vastness of the Wembley arena.

It was that, instead of an exclusion, they would race, and whoever led for the first lap would take the title of World Champion, the other would take the prize money.

When at last the tapes went up on that historic run-off, it was Langton who took the lead. He stayed ahead of Van Praag for almost the entire four laps. But on the final bend, just when it seemed the glory was to be his, the aggressive Van Praag prised him away from the inside line to flash past and take the chequered flag.

Eric Langton went down in speedway folklore as the man who lost that vital race for the sport's ultimate prize.

It was not until I approached him to ask him to talk about his career that I got a hint history may not have been, perhaps, exactly as it had seemed. It was his answer to my written question about that memorable evening which shook me.

He replied in a letter (which I still have) from his home, then in Western Australia, the final sentence of which read: 'There is a story about the 1936 Final which I am not prepared

The section of the letter in Eric's handwriting that alerted me to the possibility that all may not have been as it seemed at the 1936 World Final.

to tell. It doesn't reflect much credit on me and none at all on Van Praag. I can't tell what my feelings were then or now without divulging what happened that night at Wembley.'

It was as if I had been presented with speedway's journalistic Holy Grail. I followed up the letter with a personal phone call across the world direct to Eric who, after a great deal of persuasion, eventually gave me permission to publish his remarks.

From our conversation I was able to deduce that as the two men and officials at the starting area tried to sort out the chaos, and the massive crowd held its collective breath, Eric was approached by Van Praag with the astonishing proposition.

It has never been explained why Eric was not excluded for breaking the tapes. One theory is that the crowd may have demolished Wembley in its fury at being denied the drama of the climactic run-off. The other is that there was a sub-plot contrived by Van Praag and his Australian compatriot, Bluey Wilkinson of West Ham. I have been severely criticised in the past for disclosing what it was, but stand by every word.

It should be understood that at the time the title of World Champion held little or no significance for the stars of the track. They were much more concerned with hard cash. Bluey and Van Praag appear to have devised a scheme to extract the £500 top prize, the £250 second prize and one of them having a perfect score of 15 points on the night.

This was to be achieved by Bluey riding undefeated, which he did, and Van Praag taking the title. This could be achieved because Bluey had fewer qualifying bonus points (10) than Van Praag (12). They were points which each rider carried with him to the Final in those days.

The problem was that Eric Langton had more bonus points (13) than any of the 16 finalists. Over the meeting the other threats – England's Jack Parker, Frank Charles and George Newton *(See Page 100)* – all dropped out of the running. Eric came along and spoiled everything on the night.

For the grand plan to succeed, the two conspirators were going to have to offer Eric a deal. It was while Eric's bike was being prepared for the final run-off that Van Praag approached him.

Left: *Captain Fantastic: Eric in his Belle Vue colours, all concentration and focus, ready to race at West Ham.*
Right: *The Old Firm of Langton and Parker in their England jerseys sandwich Australia's Bluey Wilkinson in a Test at Wembley.*

For a man of Langton's high integrity – which we established earlier – the suggestion was totally incredible, utterly alien to everything he believed in. It was, after all, an invitation to conspire in a piece of sporting manipulation. Or cheating.

In spite of all that – and no doubt it is what he meant when he wrote that no credit was reflected on either of them – with the seconds ticking agonisingly away, Langton agreed.

Years later, when confronted with all this, the Van Praag version was, of course, a denial of any conspiracy. He had merely insisted he agreed to Eric being reinstated following the tape-breaking incident because he 'didn't want to win a World Championship that way' – that is by default without contesting the matter on the track. Another aspect put forward was, puzzlingly, that Eric's tapes offence cancelled out any deal anyway.

As Eric took the lead in the fateful race it may well have come to his mind that he had only to stay on his machine to become immortalised as speedway's first official genuine World Champion.

If it did, it understandably might well have caused him a momentary lapse of concentration – enough to allow Van Praag to go past him.

I have searched, unsuccessfully, for many years to try and find a detailed report of that race. There is though one item in *Speedway News* magazine's review of the meeting which asks: 'Isn't it curious how the ultimate champion did not emerge until the very last lap of the meeting?'

Curious indeed.

After the war there was an unprecedented speedway boom, but by then riding styles were changing and so was machine technology together with track surfaces from the deep cinders that Eric had known.

So he retired from racing to manage Odsal and make speedway frames, some of which still exist. In the mid-Fifties he retired to Western Australia near Perth where he restored vintage motorcycles and cars, making brief periodic returns to Britain.

Vintage Langton: Eric, who had 'somehow signed to ride for Belle Vue for ever', after cancelling a 'retirement' in 1946, was back in action at Harringay in 1947 and still scoring maximums.

On the winning side yet again: The Aces won the National Trophy for the seventh time in 1947 and Eric – still in 14th place in the World Rankings – watches Jack Parker receive the trophy from film star Jean Kent. Looking on, team mates (from left) Dent Oliver, Bill Pitcher, Wally Lloyd, Louis Lawson and Jim Boyd.

A long-retired Eric shows his trophy cabinet to his friend the late Rev. Wilf Curtis who was British speedway's official chaplain with a passion for the sport.

He said: 'I retired in 1947 when I was forty. I realised that I probably wouldn't improve much more and it was best to get out while I was still at the top. I suppose my career was successful considering the amount of money I earned and the number of trophies I won. My career was immensely satisfying.'

He once described to me his final race. It was at Hyde Road. He had a clutch cable problem and had to start off the footrest. To his chagrin he knew he had no chance then of going out in a blaze of winning glory.

'I always thought that determination was the principal characteristic in the makeup of the successful speedway rider and thought I possessed enough of that. But meeting Tommy Price (England's first World Champion in 1949) socially here in Perth recently made me realise how lacking I had been, and how well endowed with great determination he was. It carried him to the top.'

Eric died aged ninety-two in 1999. His ashes were brought home to England the following year and laid by his son Simon in his parents' plot at Farnley cemetery near Pudsey, midway between Bradford and Leeds.

Granddaughter Jennifer said of him: 'Eric is very modest and has had a very interesting and successful life. During his twenty-year speedway career he earned the title "the greatest of them all". '

Once, Eric was himself asked who he thought was the best speedway rider of all time. His response: 'Jack Parker. Of all the riders I ever saw he was the best. I had a great

friendship with Jack, and although speedway was a cut-throat business we always retained a mutual respect for each other.'

It's strange, but I once asked Jack Parker the same question: who did he consider the greatest of them all?

What he actually said was: 'Well, modestly forbids ... but no, Eric Langton. Eric had everything.'

Eric and former World Champion Tommy Price talk over old times at a get-together after they had both retired to Western Australia. Eric said that he thought he had possessed enough determination to be a successful speedway rider, 'but meeting Tommy made me realise how lacking I had been and how well endowed with determination he was. It carried him to the top'.

Ron Johnson

DOWNFALL OF A SUPERSTAR

THE MEETING OF TWO of speedway's most dynamic personalities could not have been more combustible. A 'wild sort of guy named Johnnie Hoskins' had opened the sweeping Claremont circuit in Perth, Western Australia in 1927 and given an aspiring 20-year-old named Ron Johnson his first competitive ride.

Johnnie put Ron in on a 17-second start. And after he'd won at 60 mph and earned £25 in the process, the Old Warhorse was heard to roar: 'Who's that *blankety, blank, blank* who is ruining my *blank* meeting by winning so *blank* easily?'

Young Ron and Roarin' John were on their way to speedway, and worldwide, glory. They were to experience varied circumstances on the way.

Johnnie's fluctuating fortunes were financial, but he ended up an MBE and died, venerated, at the grand old age of 95. Ron's were to do with physical injuries. He was to achieve stardom and reach the exalted heights of fabulous idolatry and success. He was also to know the very depths of despair, and to die alone and forgotten at the age of 76.

The legend of Ron Johnson is the story of one of the most skilful and shining talents among those who ever laid claim to being artists at the cinders game. Though born in Scotland, Johnson's family took him to Australia when he was six. The family name was Johnston – with a 't' – but he later dropped the 't' to make the pronunciation easier for track announcers.

'My first meeting brought me close on £50,' Ron recalled. 'It was more than I earned in a couple of months at my garage job. As can be expected, little Ron didn't go back to work any more.'

He went on to win what he described as 'a heap of silver sashes, golden gauntlets and helmets', and when Hoskins and the assault wave of early Australian pioneers headed for Europe in 1928, Ron was among them – along with such names as Vic Huxley, Frank Arthur, Dick Smythe, Charlie Datson and Sig Schlam. But at first he found it hard going on the smaller English tracks which were half the size of the huge Australian circuits he was used to.

It was ironic that the smaller tracks caused him so much trouble because, eventually, he was to become the unmatched King of the tiny south London circuit of New Cross which was only 262 yards round and became affectionately known as the Frying Pan.

But Ron did make progress and began to pull in a regular £300 a week – a fabulous equivalent to almost £9,000 a week in today's values. But the sport was, and is, a tough calling. Speedway giveth, but speedway also taketh away, and it started to exact its toll on Ron Johnson. It began to take bits of him away.

In a match race on a borrowed bike against Frank Arthur at Exeter he scraped the fence. He said: 'After finishing I looked down and saw my little toe hanging out of my boot.' In hospital he was asked if he wanted to keep the toe. It could be plastered but it would take three months to heal. 'I can't afford to wait that long,' Ron told the doctor. 'Off with it.' And off it came.

Next, racing against Vic Huxley, he reached down to his crank case to check if he was losing oil, and his primary chain whipped off

High stakes clash: Ron Johnson (outside) defending his British Championship in 1933 at Crystal Palace against West Ham's Harold 'Tiger' Stevenson.

Above left: *Home track advantage … for the challenger: Ron shakes hands with Syd Jackson before their meeting at Wimbledon. Ron kept his title.*
Above right: *On to a winner: The ten-man Australian team before the second Test of 1931 at the Leicester Super Speedway ridden on what was described as 'an appalling track' – so appalling that Ron and England's Squib Burton crashed in the first heat and Ron took no further part in the meeting. But Australia won by a single point 46 – 47. Standing from left: Lionel Van Praag, Vic Huxley, Johnnie Hoskins, Ron Johnson, Bobbie Blake, Frank Arthur, Arnie Hansen, Len Woods. Front: Max Grosskreutz, Dicky Case, Bluey Wilkinson.*

the tops of two fingers. The incident happened at Crystal Palace and it was there that he began his long association with promoters Fred Mockford and Cecil Smith, riding in the Palace team alongside such greats as Tom Farndon and George Newton.

In 1934 Mockford and Smith moved the Palace side to New Cross. In the meantime Ron had become British Champion, a match race competition, one against one, home and away with any necessary decider on a neutral track. It was then the nearest the sport had to a World Championship and was frequently advertised as such. Ron won the title from Wimbledon's Claude Rye and then promptly lost it to West Ham's Harold 'Tiger' Stevenson.

Ron was not a swashbuckler. He had a modest and withdrawn personality. It meant he rarely shone when it came to the big individual events. He explained it like this: 'My temperament is supposed by a lot of people to upset me on the big solo occasions. Well, I am a bit highly strung. I do get all het up inside. But what rider doesn't? Unfortunately I show it more than others.'

But he was never short of big occasion experience. He reached the finals of five of the seven pre-war Star Championships, finishing second in 1933 to Tom Farndon. He rode 55 times for Australia, frequently as captain, won two London Riders Championships,

Among the elite of the pre-war era, the very best of speedway at the time. Centre standing: Nobby Key, Herbert 'Dusty' Haigh, Dicky Case, Geoff Pymar, Bluey Wilkinson, Arthur Franklyn, Wal Phillips, Ron and Vic Huxley. Front: Arthur Atkinson and Tommy Croombs. Standing at the rear, Syd Jackson and pysiotherapist Nobby Clarke.

reached two of the three pre-war World Finals, all three of the immediate post-war equivalents, the British Championships, finishing second to Vic Duggan in 1948.

He qualified for the 1935 Star Final at Wembley, but the night before the meeting, in one of the greatest tragedies of his career, he was injured in the fatal accident that claimed the life of his friend and team mate Tom Farndon on their home track at New Cross.

It was as a team man that Ron was at his best. With Crystal Palace there was the London Cup in 1931 and with New Cross in 1934, 1937 and 1947. There were also league titles with New Cross in 1938 and 1948.

The Champions … New Cross won the National League title in 1938. With their trophies are, at the back standing, Clem Mitchell (in overcoat), Ron, promoter Fred Mockford and local dignitaries, Bill Longley. Sitting, Goldie Restall, Joe Francis, Stan Greatrex, Ernie Evans, Ray Duggan and Jack Milne.

Above: *Defying Hitler: Ron Johnson was one of the few overseas riders who stayed in Britain throughout the war. To help keep speedway alive and the (rather large) wartime crowds entertained, he was a regular at the wartime meetings at Belle Vue, here in a close encounter with Eric Langton.*

Below: *At the start of the most successful period of his career, leading New Cross in 1946, with, from the left, Ray Moore, Keith Harvey, Eric French, Alf Coles, team manager, Les Wotton, Frank Lawrence, Mick Mitchell. Ron is on the bike and Geoff Pymar on his back mudguard.*

Fall from grace: A 1934 report of one (of seven) of Ron Johnson's motoring misdemeanours up to that time – fined £5 and banned after crashing his car on the way to race at Plymouth. Attempts to evade the consequences failed.

His racing skills rocketed him to world class status. The small town shy boy from the Australian Outback began to mix with the social and sporting elite. Only the best was good enough for Ron Johnson at the height of his fame. He rode like a star and he lived what today would be considered the life of a superstar … with all the attendant trappings

His second wife Ruby said: 'I never discussed with him the money he made, but we lived in the Dorchester Hotel, at the time the number one hotel in London. He had his suits made at the best tailors and we ate in the best restaurants. His bikes were looked after at the track and he was idolised by the crowds. Ron was the draw card wherever he went.'

Above: But he could never quite wrest the British Match Race Championship from the Golden Helmet maestro Jack Parker, though nominated as a challenger several times. Ron lost this one in front of his home crowd and, gripping his runner's-up trophy, he forces a smile while Parker is presented with the big prize.

But it all came crashing down – literally – at Wimbledon on 1 August, 1949 in Heat 7 of a London Cup match. He was following his partner Cyril Roger for a 5-1 win when Roger got into difficulties in front of him and caused Ron to fall. Wimbledon's Cyril Brine, who was behind, rode into him and Ron suffered a fractured skull.

World class off the track living the high life in top hotels … and world class on it as well, Johnson at his very best playing the captain's role team riding with Eric French.

Left: Captain of his country, calling the shots for Australia before the third Test at New Cross in 1948, alongside England captain Jack Parker as they wait for promoter Fred Mockford's coin to reveal who gets to choose starting positions.

Middle: And the finest hour – finishing runner-up to Vic Duggan at Wembley in the Speedway Riders Championship Final, the last before the World Championship proper was restored the following year. Third placed Alec Statham is on the left.

Right: Another triumph, accepting the News Of The World *1948 National League Champion-ship trophy from the paper's editor Sir William Emsley Carr.*

Doctors told him he would have to stay in hospital for six months, but he discharged himself after a month, vowing to ride again.

The idol of the Old kent Road did ride again, but the magic had gone. At New Cross his scoring was poor. Hoskins, the man who had given him his first ride all those years ago, was running Second Division Glasgow Ashfield at the time and gave him a place in the side. But it was a disaster and Ron gave up and in 1952 returned to Australia.

Yet the lure of the track and the idolatory was too strong. After a struggle, Johnson finally got his racing licence back and, helped by former King Of Claremont and World Finalist Chum Taylor, won the 1954-55 West Australian Championship.

The great stylist: A close up of Ron Johnson's superb economy of technique easing his way past Wal Morton at Harringay.

It inspired him to return to Britain to try once more. He was given a few rides at West Ham but felt he was not given a proper chance. The good life had become as bad as it could be. His days at the Dorchester gave way to a bed-sitter off his beloved Old Kent Road. *Speedway News* magazine launched an appeal for fans to pay his far home to Australia once more.

There had been two prison sentences for drink driving. Former Birmingham captain Phil 'Tiger' Hart was with Ron on the ENSA speedway tour to entertain the forces in Europe just after the war. He told me: 'I was Ron Johnson's minder. My job was to keep him off the booze.

'What a job. You couldn't keep him away from the booze. One night in a Brussels hotel I was called downstairs at about midnight. "Mr Hart," they said, "Mr Johnson is trying to kill the hall porter." Ron had come in drunk, got into an argument with the porter and was trying to throttle him. When Johnno was drunk there was nothing he wouldn't do.'

The second time he was sent to jail the court also imposed a lifetime driving ban, and starkly described Johnson as 'almost a pathetic figure, obviously a wreck of a man because of injuries sustained while catering for public amusement … '

Of the effects of the 1949 accident he said: 'I was hopeless. I had the best machinery but I'd lost my punch. I was plagued by headaches to a tortuous degree and they affected my control.'

The ill-fated comebacks ended in a final appearance at New Cross, which had been resurrected by Hoskins with the financial aid of Phil Hart and was then in the Provincial League. On May 14, 1963 Ron met veteran Phil Bishop in a second half match race.

Five years later he was involved in a road accident which resulted in him having to use a wheelchair for the rest of his life. In 1983 the one-time hero of thousands was found alone in a house once owned by his mother. He had been dead for a week.

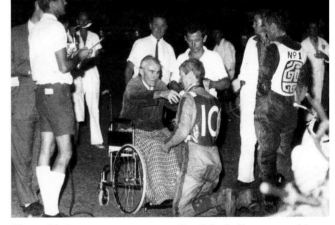

He couldn't stay away … even after it had all come crashing down, and following numerous disastrous racing comebacks, the good life was finally over for a frail Ron Johnson, wheelchair bound following a road accident. Kneeling to accept what appears to be a benediction from the former idol of thousands, five-times World Champion Ove Fundin during a meeting at Perth, Western Australia. Also in the picture immediately behind Ron Johnson is Aub Lawson, promoting there at the time, and the rider looking on is Chum Taylor.

Ron Johnson, undoubtedly one of speedway's greatest stylists, was buried in Karrakatta cemetery in Perth, Western Australia and because there was no money for a proper memorial stone he lay for ten years in an unmarked grave. Half a world away in London, one of his most devoted fans, Bob Buckingham, asked a friend to put some flowers on his hero's grave, and was horrified to learn that Ron's grave was an unmarked plot.

An appeal was launched to honour the Johnson memory, and fans and admirers from all over the world donated more than £2,000 for a proper headstone and a trophy to be competed for at a special Ron Johnson memorial meeting at the old Claremont speedway.

In the fullness of time Ron Johnson was voted by the West Australian public their 'most successful sportsman ever', and a plaque to this effect was placed on his grave.

The simple gravestone in Karrakatta cemetery.

Frank Charles
FABULOUS FRANK'S FINAL FAREWELL

THE DATE: Saturday, 15 July 1939. The place: The speedway pits at Belle Vue Manchester. Riders were concentrating their thoughts during those precious minutes before the start of the meeting, tuning themselves physically and their machines mechanically for that night's racing for the Cotton Trophy.

Among them was England's future first World Champion Tommy Price of Wembley. He was busy, in his usual thorough way, with his preparations, and totally focused on the task ahead.

Tommy recalled, years later, how he was approached by Wimbledon's Geoff Pymar. He said that by Geoff's manner he knew, somehow instinctively, that something was wrong.

Before Geoff said anything at all Tommy remembered remarking: 'It's Frank, isn't it? Something's happened to him.'

Geoff told Tommy that his Wembley team mate Frank Charles had been killed that afternoon in a glider crash.

To Tommy Price, Frank Charles was much more than a mere team mate. He was his idol, his role model and his mentor. Frank had two obsessions in life: to ride for Wembley and – never mind the world speedway title – to win the World Long Distance Gliding Championship.

The way it was at Leeds in 1931: Leicester Super are the visitors and the riders are Frank Charles, Alec Hill, Alf Somersby and Fred Wilkinson.

The sport of speedway racing, a means to finance his gliding ambitions, he could take or leave alone … and he did so on more than one occasion.

The circumstances and details of the glider accident that claimed Frank Charles's life had always remained sketchy, to say the least, until a yellowing newspaper cutting came into my possession. It was pasted to the back of a *Speedway News* magazine report of Tommy Price's 1946 Wembley triumph in the British Riders Championship Final, the substitute for the official World Championship which he was to win for England a mere three years later.

It had been sent to me with a bundle of photographs by Tommy's widow Margaret from her home in Fremantle, Western Australia.

Before I disclose what the cutting revealed about the tragedy that happened that Saturday afternoon 76 years ago, we really need to know more about the fabulous Frank Charles.

As William Shakespeare observed in *Twelfth Night*, acknowledged to be a tale of drink, dance and giving in to general self-indulgence, 'some men are born great, some achieve greatness, and some have greatness thrust upon them'.

Twelfth Night is a rollicking comedy, and comedies usually have a happy ending. But you already know that the story of Frank Charles has no happy ending.

Frank Charles was not born great. He did achieve greatness and may even have had greatness thrust upon him. Whatever, he was certainly one of England's greatest speedway riders.

To Frank Charles racing on a speedway track was a more lucrative and exciting means of earning a living than any other he tried. And he tried a few. He gave up speedway racing twice, and twice he made a comeback. Both times he was better than ever.

Now that is a rare thing in this sport of ours. You may correct me if I'm wrong, but I can recall the names of only two others who made really successful returns to the track. They are Ronnie Moore and Ove Fundin.

The boy Charles, born in Barrow-in-Furness, was 20 years old when the speedway racing phenomenon swept through the nation in exactly the same way that Beatlemania was to do four decades later. Today, of course, he would be considered a late starter. He had learned to ride motorcycles in beach races around the northern seaside resorts.

He once recalled: 'When I got to hear about the new sport I thought I might as well have a go at it. In those days I was ready to have a go at anything provided it rewarded me with a bit of fun and amusement.'

Maybe it was his apprenticeship in the beach competitions, but he appears to have been a natural speedway rider from the start. His first meeting was on the Blackpool track. 'I had never seen or ridden in a speedway race before,' said Frank, 'but I won that very first race, and with plenty to spare.'

Yet presumably all he got from that was fun and amusement because he was disqualified for looking behind.

Frank Charles was a man of numerous talents. He had started to earn his living in the family bakery business, but became bored and, as an accomplished accordian player, forsook earning dough baking bread to earning dough on the nation's music halls. In later years he would entertain the crowds from Wembley's centre green by serenading them during the intervals at speedway meetings.

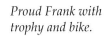

Proud Frank with trophy and bike.

But he tired of showbusiness as well, because he performed mostly at cinemas and found it tedious having to sit through the same films night after night waiting to go on.

Speedway had become as popular in the north as it had in the south and the lure of the track was too strong for Frank. He was soon thrilling the crowds at Manchester White City, Belle Vue, Burnley, Preston and Leeds.

For company he had some of the sport's other great northern stars such as Harry Riley 'Ginger' Lees, Gordon Byers, Eric Langton, Frank Varey, Herbert 'Dusty' Haigh, Walter Hull and Bob Harrison.

It was a time in the speedway scheme of things when the divide between the north and south was such that they kept themselves very much to themselves.

But in 1930 a crunch match was arranged between Wembley from the south and cock's-o'-the-north Belle

The amazing pre-war Belle Vue side, the all-conquering Aces who won twenty one team trophies between 1933 and 1939: From the left Frank 'El Diablo Rojo' Varey, Max Grosskreutz, Bob Harrison, Eric Langton, Joe 'Iron Man' Abbott, Bill Kitchen, Frank Charles. In front young mascot Bob Staye.

Above left: *Test action at New Cross in 1935, Frank out front ahead of Dicky Case, Vic Huxley and Joe Abbott.*

Above right: *Riding to the rescue ... of Wembley. It cost a record £1,000 in transfer money but for Frank putting on the famous Lions sweater and racing in the Empire Stadium was an ambition achieved.*

Vue for the right to the title of British Champions. Wembley won and it may have been this that fired Frank's ambition to one day ride for Wembley.

The following year, when he had become known as a rider of high quality, he was with Leeds at the old Leicester Super speedway when, perhaps inevitably, he was involved in a bad crash. It affected his appetite for the sport and he went back to the family bakery business. He was to be away from the track for a couple of seasons until Belle Vue hit an injury crisis and the club's shrewd boss E.O. Spence persuaded Frank to climb back aboard a bike.

In doing so Spence created the marvellous Belle Vue winning colossus that earned the respect of speedway the world over and became recognized as the greatest club side on earth.

During the middle Thirties, between 1933 and 1936, the Aces carried everything before them, winning the league and National Trophy double four years running. Many of today's chroniclers (perhaps conveniently) forget those high achievement days in the history of Belle Vue because they do not have a mind to research further back than 1965, the start of the so-called modern era and the British League.

In those middle pre-war seasons Bill Kitchen and Australia's Max Grosskreutz had arrived on the scene and, for part of the time, Frank Charles formed a formidable partnership with little Joe Abbott, the 'Iron Man', so-called because of the many times he fought back from devastating injuries. They were the scourge, not only of other league pairings, but of their international rivals as well.

'They were great days,' Frank said. 'But even they began to pall after a time and I began to get impatient again. I needed a change, so I went into the grocery business.'

It may not have been as simple a choice as that. In 1934 Frank's father died. Charles senior, it is reported, was an outstanding mechanic and went with his son to nearly all his meetings. One account says that Frank's Dad was so good a mechanic that his son 'could boast the distinction of having had his engines measured by the authorities on more occasions than any other rider.'

Once again, Frank soon realized that life in the grocery trade was even duller than being a baker and it so happened that early in 1935, way down south, Wembley had been struck by a similar injury crisis as had Belle Vue in 1933.

The Lions' captain, Colin Watson, and Frank's old pal Ginger Lees were both out of action. Watson broke a leg at West Ham when it was knocked into his chain. The injury was so bad that it was thought to be the end of the career of the veteran, who had been in the game since day one in 1928. It wasn't, Watson did race again, ironically for West Ham.

The West Ham hoodoo also struck Lees who crashed into the fence and was expected to be out for some time. It was even rumoured that he was considering retiring to concentrate on his garage business in Bury.

To make the situation in the Lions' den even more critical for manager Alec Jackson, Wembley had publicly announced that they had signed one of the biggest stars in the sport, Cyclone Billy Lamont who had missed the previous British season. The trouble was that by midway through April The Cyclone had failed to arrive at the Empire Stadium from his native Australia.

So Jackson drove the 300 miles to Barrow to try and persuade Frank to help Wembley out. When Jackson got there, Frank was in bed with flu so, not wishing to disturb him too much, he said why he had come and immediately drove the 300 miles back to London.

The following day Frank sent a telegram which read: 'Alec, will ride for Wembley when fit, perhaps in two weeks.' Alec Jackson couldn't have known it, but Frank had achieved one of his ambitions.

The transfer deal Jackson struck with Spence at Belle Vue was that Frank could ride for Wembley in 1935,

and if they wanted to keep him in 1936 his transfer fee would be based on performance.

It was thought that this was likely to be the highest in the history of the sport – probably somewhere near four figures. It was. Frank Charles was eventually transferred to Wembley from Belle Vue for £1,000. A record for the time and – as near as dammit – the equivalent of £35,000 now.

Frank's first appearance for Wembley was against Harringay. He scored five points, in spite of the lingering effects of flu and one broken chain. But he was off and flying again in no time after that, particularly when it came to taking on his old Belle Vue pals.

Barely a fortnight after his return to the track he was named in the England side for the first Test against the Australians at Wembley at the beginning of June. He scored a vital 11 points in England's 56 – 52 victory, a performance more than justifying his transfer fee.

He said: 'I believe that my transfer fee was the largest ever paid for a speedway rider. Of course, it is absurd to place my ability at such a huge figure, but the fact that it is valued so highly certainly inspired me to ride as hard as I knew how and prove my worth. And I had realized one of my ambitions. I was a Wembley Lion.'

But the best was yet to come.

The grand climax of Frank's comeback, probably of his career, came at the end of August, fittingly at Wembley Stadium, when he won what really was a World Championship in everything but name. He rode to an immaculate 15-point maximum in the last Star Championship Final. The following year the official FIM World Championship was launched.

That year the old match race formula for the competition had been replaced with a brand new idea – 16 riders meeting each other once over 20 heats in what was to become the classic five-ride championship format.

Back in the Belle Vue pits as a visitor with the Wembley team: From left the 1936 Lions are Wally Lloyd, Eric Gregory, Frank, Alec Jackson, manager, Ginger Lees, Gordon Byers and George Greenwood. At the front Cliff Parkinson and Lionel Van Praag.

Best pair ... fun-loving Frank gives wife Doris a ride round Wembley.

Life at the top, leading England before the second Test at Wembley in 1938. Lined up from the left: Arthur Atkinson, George Newton, Frank Varey, Bill Kitchen, Tommy Croombs and Frank. At the back Geoff Pymar and the unseen George Wilks.

Tragedy had hung over the big night. The previous evening reigning British Champion Tom Farndon, probably the world's best at that time, had been involved in a bad accident with his New Cross team mate Ron Johnson on the Old Kent Road track and within days had died of his injuries.

Even without Farndon and Johnson, who was also injured in the crash, the Star field was formidable: Eric Langton, Bluey Wilkinson, Jack Parker, Vic Huxley, Dick Case, Tiger Stevenson, Jack Ormston, Max Grosskreutz, Lionel Van Praag and Bill Kitchen were there. All were world class and all were more race fit than Frank.

He clinched the title in a climactic Heat 14 when, in *Boys' Own Paper* hero style, he brilliantly outrode the also previously unbeaten Ormston and Max.

The following season Frank made more history by winning the opening race of the sport's first World Final, of course at Wembley, setting a new track record of 73.6 seconds. His Wembley captain Van Praag also made history by winning that first Final, Frank finishing fourth jointly with America's Cordy Milne.

But there was that other ambition waiting to be fulfilled. That gliding championship. Frank called it his hobby, but he took it very seriously indeed. 'Like every other rider,' he confessed, 'I should like to win the World Championship, but I am far more concerned with beating gliding records. And I must say that if I can earn enough on the speedway to be able to build thousands of gliders, I shall be satisfied.'

While at Wembley Frank had taken a special interest in the struggling young Tommy Price, then in the early stages of his career. Frank had coaxed Tommy out of trailing his left leg and into adopting the more modern foot-forward style of riding. It was as a result of Frank's teaching that Tommy went on to much greater things.

Tommy became very fond of Frank, so much so that he not only had that premonition in the Belle Vue pits on the evening of July 15, but his wife Margaret later confessed to me that he had been devastated to learn that Frank had been killed in what amounted to a freak accident.

Frank had been selected for the England side for the Harringay Test that night, but had asked to be excused from his international duties so that he could take part in the gliding competition.

Just forty-eight hours earlier he had inspired his Lions to the narrowest two point win over West Ham in a National Trophy match at the Empire Stadium. His final ride had been an epic struggle with the brilliant Arthur Atkinson in Heat 15. Right to the last bend Frank had pressured the Hammers' star, the pair treating the fans to a classic speedway duel, and the big crowd had loved it. It was the stuff of which real speedway was – and is – made. The Lions supporters had cheered Frank madly, even though he lost the race narrowly.

As he cruised slowly back to the pits Frank, beneath his red helmet, stood on his footrest, turned and raised an arm high in acknowledgment, saluting the packed stands in return.

It was to be his final farewell.

Gliding had become such an obsession that when Frank joined Wembley he had moved his home from Barrow to near Dunstable, In Bedfordshire, where Dunstable Downs, then as now, was a well known ideal gliding area.

The National Gliding competition which so enthralled him was held at Great Hucklow, Derbyshire. Frank recognized the dangers. There had been crashes before – one particularly hazardous one near Barrow when his plane landed on the edge of cliff in a quarry.

Details of the one that killed him on 15 July 1939 are contained in the 75 words of that yellowing newspaper cutting. Previous reports had merely recounted how the tow line had failed to fall from Frank's glider and it had nosedived into the ground from 300 feet.

The headline on that small cutting was: DOG KILLS SPEED ACE IN GLIDER.

And this is what I read:

FRANK CHARLES Wembley speedway star killed during the national gliding competitions at Great Hucklow, Derbyshire, on Saturday, crashed in a field in which his two sons were playing.

When Charles's glider was launched a dog became entangled in the towing wire and was lifted into the air.

The winch stopped, and the dog got free. But the glider went on until the wire tightened and dragged its nose down. The glider then somersaulted and crashed.

Frank Charles died in front of his own sons. How poignant ... how sad ... is that?

Tragedy. The newspaper report of Frank's bizarre fatal accident during the gliding competition.

The headstone on Frank's grave recording the date of the disaster ... and he was only thirty-two years old.

Geoff Mardon
OFFERS THE KIWIS COULDN'T REFUSE

THE GREAT BRITISH SPEEDWAY public was told by the great British speedway Press 'to expect an invasion by a new batch of Anzacs … Starters include Spike Jones, Mick Holland, Barry Stormont, Julie Benson, possibly Merv Neil and Jeff Marden'.

And the great British speedway Press took to speculating whether the Anzacs would turn up another Ronnie Moore or Ron Johnston?' *(See Page 118)*

It was little more than a throwaway line on page six of *Stenner's Speedway Annual 1951*. And the author, E.W.Sullivan, who had been reviewing the season in New Zealand, got at least one name wrong – it should have been Mardon, not Marden. And the first name should have been Geoff, not Jeff.

Wally Kilmister had blazed the trail for New Zealand pre-war with Wembley, reaching the 1935 Star Final, then the nearest speedway had to a World Championship. Since 1947 big Harold Fairhurst had been a useful regular with Second Division Glasgow and Edinburgh where Dick Campbell was top of the heap. And Jackie Hunt at Newcastle promised much until injury in 1948 halted his progress.

In 1950 Moore had arrived sensationally at Wimbledon and Johnston at Belle Vue. But some other New Zealanders who had served their apprenticeship in the Third Division were starting to put the little country at the other end of the world on the speedway map.

From Rayleigh Bruce Abernethy had finally made it to Wembley, and his team mate Maury Dunn was on his way up to Harringay. Trevor Redmond was also Wembley bound from Aldershot. Julie Benson found his way to Rayleigh, Mick Holland to Cardiff and Merv Neil eventually to Norwich.

Of Spike Jones and Barry Stormont there is no trace. And no one had even heard of Barry Briggs or Ivan Mauger outside of their native land.

The question E.W. Sullivan asked came nearest to being answered by the man whose name he got wrong. The entire speedway world was searching for another Ronnie Moore at the time – and Geoff Mardon seemed determined to prove that lightning can strike twice in the same place.

A very talented New Zealand line-up at Aranui in 1958: Geoff, on the left, and Barry Briggs, on the far right, had long established themselves at Wimbledon, but Ivan Mauger, centre, was still struggling.

Above left: *The Wimbledon National Trophy winning side of 1953, described as 'a team of fiery fighters', from the left: Reg Trott, Barry Briggs, Cyril Maidment, Norman Parker (on bike), Cyril Brine, Peter Moore, Geoff, Ronnie Moore and Don Perry.*

Above right: *The immaculate Mardon all-action style.*

In his first season in Britain with Third Division Aldershot he qualified for the World Final. As Ronnie had with First Division Wimbledon the year before. Though Geoff was only second reserve on the big night at Wembley, he is – and remains – the only Third Division rider to reach such dizzy heights.

It doesn't get much more sensational than that. But Wembley on September 20, 1951 was a night packed with sensation upon sensation, as well as high drama, so it was understandable perhaps that the great British speedway Press didn't make as much as they might have done of a virtual unknown from Christchurch.

The most illustrious of those who came after, the six times World Champion Ivan Mauger, said of Geoff: 'Because Ronnie and later Briggo won the World Championship a lot of people do not seem to know that Geoff was the first New Zealander to get on the podium when he was third in 1953. In my opinion he retired prematurely. I think he could have improved on that third place.'

The thing was, Goff Mardon, a young carpenter, had no ambitions to reach the speedway heights at all. He says: 'I was not really attracted to speedway. I would have preferred to go road racing. To this end I bought an AJS 7R on time payment. I soon found out that road racing costs money, which I didn't have, while speedway paid. So it was not a tough decision.'

Although at the time, as Ivan Mauger has said, 'we all wanted to be like Ronnie', Geoff says: 'I just wanted to do well.' And he looked in only one direction for inspiration, to the visiting veteran English international Norman Parker, captain of Wimbledon, who originally saw the potential in Ronnie Moore and took him back to Plough Lane.

To begin with Geoff's progress was hindered by inferior equipment and a riding style that, reportedly, 'would condemn him to mediocrity and despair'.

He was a good old fashioned leg-trailer. And his early efforts were not appreciated. He says: 'I was considered a menace to other riders on the track and was banned until I changed my style. I started as a leg-trailer because my first bike was home built based on an old Rudge road frame, with front forks from a 1912 Thor motoryle, similar to a Harley-Davidson, and it felt natural to leg-trail.'

But the driving force that made him determined to carry on was simple, he says: 'I didn't want to be seen as a fool. I still had no money so I photographed some modern frames and built what I considered a copy. Strangely, it seemed to work and I soon found I was in the Christchurch team.'

In an article about Geoff in a 1996 issue of the old *Vintage Speedway Magazine*, fellow New Zealander and former Newcastle star Ivan Crozier described how Ronnie and Geoff watched and learned from the other touring English riders, practising hour after hour and investing all the cash they could scrape together to pay for methanol and mechanical wear and tear.

Geoff says: 'Norm Parker was always someone I wanted to emulate. I watched him and realized he went into the corners faster than me, so next time I was out with him I decided that I wouldn't shut off till after he did. That was the best lesson I ever learned as I found I had more control. Parker's coaching was rubbing off on all of us and a lot of things began to come together.'

The man who could be described as New Zealand speedway's Godfather, the late Trevor Redmond, was the only local rider able to get near the English experts. Geoff said: 'What Norm Parker did for me was teach me how to stay with Redmond. I couldn't beat him, but

I could stay with him. At the end of 1951 I began to pass him.'

Geoff paid a glowing tribute to the rotund Redmond who became affectionately known throughout the sport as 'Fats': 'Without Trevor Redmond I would never have had the confidence to go to England,' he said. 'He arranged a trial at Aldershot, organized a place to stay and an old Chrysler car we shared for transport. Any success I had in England is all due to him.'

Crozier reported that to get to England Geoff sold everything he had – his carpentry tools, his road bike and his speedway bike. He arrived in Aldershot in the clothes he stood up in and a duffle bag with a helmet, a set of American field boots and a two-piece set of home made leathers. He and Redmond slept in 30-bob-a-week digs.

Early reports of his progress at Aldershot suggested that he was 'seriously ambitious' but once again held back by poor equipment, and less than adequate leathers.

Geoff has a completely different slant on how things were at that time. He says: 'My equipment at Aldershot was all new and well maintained by Mike Erskine. Third Division sounds a bit down market but there were many riders who could hold their own in more exalted company.'

Indeed there were. Bob Roger was at Exeter, Alan Smith at Plymouth, Ken Middleditch at Poole, Gerald Jackson at Rayleigh, and Cyril Maidment at Wolverhampton. And as for the suggestion that, as part of that company, he was 'fiercely ambitious', he says: 'I always wanted to do well, but ambitious to the extreme…NO.'

Nevertheless, Redmond and Mardon carried Aldershot to third place in the league table behind Poole and Exeter. Reviews of the season described the section as 'the healthiest league' and commented: 'In only their second season Aldershot struck lucky again with a young New Zealand rider. Geoff Mardon was little behind Trevor Redmond when it came to scoring.'

And this: 'Aldershot … again produced a rider of unusual ability. In 1950 it was Redmond. This time it was Geoff Mardon, another New Zealander.' In that year's Third Division rankings, their performances earned Redmond second place behind Middleditch and Geoff was at number four, one behind Alan Smith.

There was a footnote. It said: 'This time the Shots couldn't hold on and Mardon was sold to Wimbledon at a fee of over £1,000 just before the close of the season.'

So what kind of approach was there from Wimbledon? Or was it a cash carrot dangled in front of the Aldershot management? If so, what was the deal?

Geoff says: 'I was not approached by anyone. The first I knew was when the Aldershot manager told me about a Wimbledon offer of £1,000. It was then increased to £1,050, £1,000 for Aldershot and £50 for me. I felt it was a step up the ladder so I agreed to the transfer.'

Wimbledon boss Ronnie Greene had obviously made Aldershot – and Geoff – an offer

Geoff takes his place in the grand parade before the 1954 World Championship at Wembley. It was his third appearance in a Final but the tension is showing all along the line, even among the veterans. From left: Arthur Forrest, Ronnie Moore whose night it was, Geoff, Aub Lawson, Ove Fundin, Brian Crutcher, Eddie Rigg and Peter Craven.

they couldn't refuse. But the Shots lost their top two, because Wembley made 'Godfather' Redmond an offer *he* also couldn't refuse.

The clincher that made Geoff such a target for Wimbledon was his World Championship performance. It was unheard of for someone from the Third Division to ride his way through all the qualifing rounds *AND* get to a Wembley Final.

Nominated from Round One as reserve, Geoff collected 25 points in Round Two alongside such top names as Johnnie Reason of Coventry, Wimbledon's American star Ernie Roccio, Phil Clarke of Norwich, the veteran Fleetwood number one Wilf Jay, Southampton's Roy Craighead and Bristol's Jack Mountford.

In the Championship Round, at Wimbledon on August 13, Geoff scored 12 points, proving he could ride the track. It put him in joint third place on the night with Jack Young from Second Division Edinburgh. And, interestingly, Geoff had done better than his old idol, track expert Norman Parker, who was two behind him on 10. Harringay's Split Waterman won with a 15 point maximum from Ronnie Moore on 14. Truly Geoff had proved himself in world class company.

His other round, at New Cross two days later, was a meeting that included English internationals Dick Bradley of Bristol, Belle Vue's Dent Oliver and also Old Kent Road experts Cyril Roger, Jeff Lloyd and Eric French.

As if sounding another warning to the international stars of the First Division that this was to be the year their status was under threat from below, young Australian sensation Bob Leverenz of Second Division Norwich won the round on 14 points. Geoff was by no means outclassed in joint sixth place. But his nine points, though putting him above such distinguished non-qualifiers as Wembley captain Bill Kitchen, Blond Bombshell Graham Warren of Birmingham, Bristol skipper Billy Hole and the emerging Olle Nygren of Sweden, were enough to get him to the World Final only as reserve with Bradley.

A tricky situation at Belle Vue with fellow New Zealander Ron Johnston whose robust challenge has forced Geoff to lift his foot clear of the machinery.

His progress was not merely remarkable for the time, it also did his financial situation no harm at all. But what about equipment? Suddenly he was competing at the highest level – where did the necessary mechanical power and reliability come from?

Geoff says: 'Reaching the Final came as a big surprise to me, as it did to others. My equipment was the same as at Aldershot, maintained still by Mike Erskine to whom I will be eternally grateful. A real nice guy and a gentleman.'

Wembley on World Final night that year was a 93,000-spectator ordeal – trauma, more like – for a young man from what Ronnie Moore has described to me more than once as 'sleepy Christchurch'. After all, the majesty and sheer immensity of the theatre of sporting dreams has been known to be so intimidating as to make strong men weak and reduce seasoned professionals to pale and quivering wrecks.

What thoughts and emotions still linger for Geoff over the near six and a half decades since that magic night in the world's most famous sporting arena? And how did he prepare himself for such a major meeting?

He says: 'I was apprehensive to the extreme, and felt I did not belong there. As for preparation, I just hoped to not be embarrassed.'

If he did have the jitters they were never allowed an opportunity to affect his performance. Nor was he in any danger of being embarrassed. Geoff didn't get a ride. His fellow reserve, Dick Bradley, did, in Heat 18 replacing Ernie Roccio and finishing second to Louis Lawson.

As it was, Geoff had a view from the pits of the drama of Australia's Jack Biggs winning his first four rides and then failing, not once but twice, to take the title. The single point that would have made him World Champion was denied him in Heat 19, and then again in the three-man run-off for first place. He lost to Young and Waterman after they had all finished the night on 12 points. Young made history that night by becoming the first Second Division rider to take the sport's supreme prize.

Geoff's baptism into big time league speedway for Wimbledon in 1952 found him with the daunting prospect of being paired with Ronnie Moore. He said: 'It meant I was thrown in at the deep end and was riding against two heat leaders rather than one heat leader

Geoff takes command of the inside in this Wimbledon sandwich, with partner Ronnie Moore on the outside and Fred Williams having to work hard to try and force a way through the middle.

and a second string. They did everything they could to stop Ronnie. I was the muggins – the meat in the sandwich.'

His survival plan was to give as good as he got. He said: 'We were riding at Belle Vue and Dent Oliver came under me as I went into a corner and really hit me hard. I took his weight and wondered what the dickens was going on.

'Then my handlebar ripped all his front wheel spokes out, and Oliver actually looped over the top of me without touching me. I didn't know what was happening – but I got a lot of respect after that. People were very polite to me. It was nice.'

Wimbledon finished mid-table that year, and Geoff was third top scorer for the Dons behind Ronnie and Cyril Brine. He returned to Christchurch for the winter and, sensibly thinking about his financial future, was undecided about another season in Europe. But Ronnie Greene knew a thing or two about handling his riders. He telephoned Geoff in New Zealand and, according to Crozier, 'reminded him that the Holy Grail was waiting. He talked financial incentive and he talked numbers'.

Geoff said: 'The First Division was full of very fast riders who had taken years to work themselves up the ladder. They knew every gearing on every track that mattered. They knew all about the track surfaces on any one day. It was like they had risen from cabin boy to admiral the "accepted way, old boy".

'But I decided I would go back to Blighty for one more go at it … the last tilt.' It was a decision that was to earn him his own place in speedway history.

In 1953 Wimbledon had three heat leaders from New Zealand, Ronnie, Geoff and a Barry Briggs, who was fast maturing from the wild man who had joined the team the previous year.

This time Geoff's World Championship qualifying 24 points were enough to get him a ride at Wembley on Final night. It was a formidable line-up and included, Split Waterman, Fred Williams *(See Page 150)*, Jack Young, Arthur Forrest, Aub Lawson, Brian Crutcher, Graham Warren and Alan Hunt *(See Page 77)* plus two Swedes, Olle Nygren and Rune Sormander.

Modestly, Geoff says now it was 'once again a surprise to be there'. And he went on: 'We picked Ronnie to win this one – he was very fast. He was only 20 and had a string of track records under his belt. Even Briggo picked Ronnie.'

Geoff went to the tapes with Ronnie, Nygren and Eric Williams in his first ride, Heat 4. As if that was not enough pressure, rain had made the track greasy. It was a disaster for Ronnie, and a major upset to lay before the 90,000 crowd. He fell, and Geoff went on to win. Two heats later he was second to Waterman but ahead of Crutcher and Warren.

His third ride, against Lawson, Hunt and Dick Bradley was re-run after an unsatisfactory start, but he won. And after three rides he was up with the leaders, the unbeaten Fred Williams and Waterman.

From Heat 12 to 16 the starting gate refused to function and races had to be started on the green light. Geoff was out in Heat 13, and the crowd was in for another shock. The unfancied Jeff Lloyd got the better of Fred Williams with Geoff in third place ahead of Forrest.

All three Wimbledon New Zealanders were there for the 1959 World Final – Briggs, Moore and Mardon. Moore took the title for a second time in spite of a niggling leg injury, Geoff was recovering from a broken jaw and finished in tenth place, Briggs got on the rostrum in third place.

There was then an agonising seven heat wait until his last ride in Heat 20. Meanwhile, Waterman won Heat 15, setting up a Heat 17 crunch race with both Nygren and Williams to decide the title. The starting gate was back in business and Williams won to take his second world title. A win for Waterman would have given him a 15-point maximum, but he struggled in third with a clutch problem.

As second placed Nygren and Williams rode side-by-side back to the pits Olle leaned over and said: 'Freddie, I fix Split.'

A last ride win put Geoff into a run-off with Nygren for third place. He got the better of Nygren's fellow Swede Sormander, Dent Oliver and outgoing champion Jack Young. A win would have put Young in a run-off with Waterman for second place, but a fall wrecked his chances.

Of the run-off with Nygren Geoff said: 'I made a blinder of a gate and hung on as close to the pole line as I could. Olle tried everything, apparently – he hit me twice – but over-cooked it on the final bend and fell.

'It was quite a thrill to have my prize handed to me by Sir Edmund Hillary, another Kiwi who had just climbed Mt. Everest.'

Though Young was still ranked No.1 in the world with Moore second and Waterman third, Geoff's performance earned him seventh place behind Fred Williams, Olle Nygren and Aub Lawson. The 1954 season saw him better than anyone at Wimbledon – better than Moore and Briggs – and second highest scorer in the league with 274 points, only three behind top man Eddie Rigg of Odsal Bradford.

All three Wimbledon New Zealanders qualified for a World Final that heralded the dawning of a new era with the debuts of Briggs, Peter Craven and Ove Fundin. With Moore they were to dominate the World Championship for the next decade.

Fundin recalls: 'It was my first Final. I was very nervous and too much in awe of Ronnie Moore and Jack Young, so didn't really notice Geoff. He was very kind to me when I went to New Zealand. He was racing cars then and he took Ronnie and Barry and me in this great monster he drove, out to the racing circuit and we were allowed to have a go in it. As a person he is the greatest friend anyone could wish for.'

The 1954 Final was not Geoff's night. Moore, who only eight weeks before had been lying in a Danish hospital with a broken leg thinking his season was over, rode to a faultless 15-point maximum for his first world title. Geoff managed a mere five, and at the end of the night the newly crowned World Champion, with a £500 cheque in his pocket, confessed: 'I borrowed threepence from Geoff Mardon to phone my landlady.'

It was a season, Geoff admits, when he just 'decided to stay out of trouble'. The year before he had become engaged to Val Moore, Ronnie's sister, and in 1954 they married. Geoff says: 'I had seen other married overseas riders come to the UK, living in digs and rumours getting back to the wife (true or false), all adding to rows and divorce. I didn't want that.'

Ronnie Greene had paid their air fares back to London for the 1955 season, but, said Geoff: 'I turned to Val and asked her if it was all worth it. She had been on the road as far back as she could remember (with the Moore family wall of death bike show). She had

Above left: *Rivals but pals: Alan 'Whacker' Hunt gets friendly with Ronnie Moore, left, and Geoff before a Wimbledon and visiting Birmingham confrontation.*
Above right: *Veteran Kiwi and pre-war Wembley star Wally Kilmister discusses tactics with his New Zealand Test team. Paying close attention are Mick Holland, Bruce Abernethy, Ronnie Moore and Geoff.*

never said a thing about us going to London – I'd never even asked her.

'So we unpacked. I sold my four bikes and my leathers and bought a set of golf clubs. It was over. It was all over.'

But it wasn't. Quite.

Four years later Geoff turned up again in England – to ride for Southampton after a furious row was resolved between Greene at Wimbledon and the enterprising Charlie Knott at Southampton. He says: 'In 1959 Southampton got in touch with me and offered air fares, a bike and transport. So I thought OK, even if I don't cut it I can hop on a plane and go home. Nothing lost.'

The promotorial disagreement over his services he let go over his head. 'I just left them to sort it out,' he said. His form was good, second in the Saints' scoring list to Brian Crutcher and well above the emerging Swedish star and future World Champion Bjorn Knutsson. And he qualified for his fourth World Final – all this in spite of a bad crash in which his jaw was fractured.

'The Final that year was a disaster,' he says. 'I had a bad smash three weeks before the big night and spent two weeks in hospital. On top of that Charlie Knott promised me a brand new engine if I reached the Final. Unfortunately, in my second race a rocker broke in the new motor so it was back to the track spare and not a lot of incentive to try hard.'

He ended in tenth place on six points. But at least the title was back in the family. It was brother-in-law Ronnie Moore's second World Championship.

And that really was it as far as speedway was concerned. Well, no, not exactly. Geoff won the New Zealand solo championship in 1963 after finishing third the previous year behind the Old Firm, Barry Briggs and Ronnie Moore.

But mostly he raced cars. He says: 'Between 1954 and 1959 I bought a taxi business and raced a six litre sports car and a Formula 5000 single seater. Been married now more than 60 years, three children, four grandchildren. Slowed up quite a lot.'

Geoff and Val, who both still play golf to a high standard, were in England just a few years ago to look up old speedway friends and to be guests at the World Speedway Riders' Association annual dinner.

Val says of her family association with the sport: 'Sure I've worried over the years. But I've had motorbikes to deal with my whole life – my dad, my brother, my husband, my son. Our son David has six bikes for all types of off-road riding. You have to accept the risks. When your time's up you could be doing anything like crossing the road.

'We still have dinner when sometimes the talk does get onto bikes, cars and motors. It's all just memories now. Geoff and I have had a wonderful life together and are still enjoying it.'

You get a clue how true that is from the fact that part of their e-mail address is: paradise.

Geoff and Val: Still going strong after sixty years.

Dressed in their wedding finery instead of racing leathers they don't look totally comfortable. The day in 1954 that Geoff married Valerie, Ronnie's sister, and they become brothers-in-law. Val describes who is who: 'The Rev. Thorpe (now deceased), Bridesmaids Thea Withy (Scott), Carol Thomas (Spafford) and Lynne Withy (Robey). The church was St John's. It was a very pretty church but the recent earthquake saw the end of that and now there is a church built of cardboard on the site. Sounds weird and there was a lot of controversy over the building of it as it has replaced our beautiful cathedral in the heart of the city. We had our sixtieth wedding anniversary and all the wedding party were here except Lynne as she lives in USA.'

Bill Kitchen

THE LION KING...

BILL KITCHEN'S MONUMENT TO FAME

THE TUMULTUOUS ROAR of adulation that rolled round the vast terraces of the Empire Stadium as 75,000 voices greeted each member of the Wembley Lions speedway team on summer Thursday nights just after the war was enough to make any sporting hero light in the head. And turn his knees to jelly.

At that time, riders were using dressing rooms at one end of the arena and the racing pits were at the other. To get there every member of the side had to walk the entire length of that fabled football pitch in full view of the fans who idolised them.

None was more idolised than veteran skipper Bill Kitchen. Star-struck novice Eric Williams, later to become a fully-fledged Lion, international and World Finalist, described what it was like. He was visiting brother Fred, then a humble reserve but whose two world titles were not all that far in the future.

Eric said: 'When I arrived in the dressing rooms, my big brother hero was already dressed in his leathers, with the colourful Lions body colour strapped round his chest, and carrying his crash helmet and steel shoe. Fred said: "Hang on Eric, we'll follow Kitch across." What an experience this was. Kitch was a fellow so much admired in speedway racing, and simply adored by the Wembley supporters. I was already aware of the hum of the huge crowd, but when they saw Kitch come into view the whole world seemed to explode with noise.

'Until that moment, this elderly looking character was just an ordinary human being. But the second he stepped into that huge stadium, where there appeared to be a million people, he took on the status of a legend. There was the most frightening noise from those huge rattles and piercing police whistles. Everyone was screaming for Bill. I was awestruck.

'He was hobbling along because of the unusual boot on his left foot, acknowledging the incredible applause from this huge crowd as we walked the full length of Wembley's famous football field. I'll always remember how I felt on that occasion, out in the centre of a wondrous stadium with the crowd expressing its adulation of their idol Bill Kitchen.'

Bill Kitchen would have been one hundred and seven this year. Speedway posterity reveres him, not for the major individual titles he came so close to winning, but as the brilliant post-war captain of Wembley and for his unselfish endeavours on behalf of lesser team mates. An appreciation of his track career many years ago ended with these words: 'Team work is Bill Kitchen's monument to fame.' It should have been his epitaph.

There is an old music hall song that goes: 'Why am I always the bridesmaid, never the blushing bride?' It is a lament for all those who seem destined to be forever the runner-up and never quite the top achiever. It could have been Bill Kitchen's signature tune.

He died a few months short of his eighty-sixth birthday in May 1994. So he missed any

Monument to a magnificent past, one of the famous, late and very much lamented Wembley twin towers under which for so long Bill Kitchen paraded his skill and artistry.

centenary celebrations … and the telegram from the Queen. His distinguished racing career lasted twenty-one years and he was a true international, representing England in Britain and overseas in 39 Tests, many times as captain. Fred Williams credits Bill's forays into Scandinavia just after the war as laying the foundations for Denmark's later dominance of modern world speedway.

It is an enviable legacy to leave behind.

Bill Kitchen was a legend in every sense. But modest with it. If you had been skipper of the world's most famous speedway team, led them to seven league championships in eight seasons, plus numerous other honours, and for all of that time your home track had been the planet's most famous sporting arena, the Mecca of the speedway world, Wembley Stadium, you would think that magnificent effigy to excellence would merit at least a passing glance when you happened to pass it by in later years, even when your glory days were done.

Which is why I was astonished when Bill Kitchen, who was sitting opposite me in a carriage on the Metropolitan Line Tube train, didn't even acknowledge the existence of the place as we sped by it through the Middlesex suburbs of London. It couldn't have escaped his notice because those iconic twin towers were lit up like Christmas trees, and the great banks of floods bathing the interior in a golden glow silhouetted the entire incredible sporting monument in the twilight.

Kitchen the consummate captain exuding a confidence that inspired his team of Wembley Lions to such unprecedented success.

With the bright, sparkling vision whizzing by just outside the window, I had expected some sort of reaction. Isn't it everyone's impossible dream to one day strut their competitive stuff within Wembley's sacred portals, let alone demonstrate how very, very good they are at their chosen sport?

I said to Bill: 'Don't you even look at the place when you go by?'

I got a one word answer. 'No!' There was no explanation. And, incredibly – because I was overawed – I didn't ask for one. Now, looking back, I like to think that what I took that day to be apathy was really an example of Bill Kitchen's innate modesty.

But then Bill was a Lancastrian. They are as blunt as their great Yorkshire rivals. Once, when the emperor of the Empire Stadium, Sir Arthur Elvin, had shown Bill round the place after manager Alec jackson had astutely plucked him from the 1946 riders' pool to lead the Lions in the first post-war racing season, the great man made the mistake of asking Bill what he thought of the Wembley track.

Bill told him.

Sharing the National Trophy spoils with Belle Vue in 1933, the first of five consecutive victories for the northerners. The smiling Aces are, from left Max Grosskreutz, Joe Abbott, Eric Langton, mascot Bob Staye, Oliver Langton, Frank Varey with the trophy and Bill. Ironically the team is parading their win at the Empire Stadium after defeating Wembley which Bill was to lead so well after the war.

As a member of the all-conquering pre-war Belle Vue side, young Bill had ridden Wembley no end of times in the later Thirties before hostilities put a stop to league speedway. His visits included two World Finals. Bill told Sir Arthur that

Above left:
Sergeant Bill
Kitchen doing his bit
to entertain the
British occupying
forces in Europe
with the ENSA
speedway tour. Bill
is on the outside
with Wilf Plant in
the centre and
Malcolm Craven
nearest the 'starter'
who was operating a
hi-tech elastic band.

Above right:
Before the second in
the 1938 Test series,
Bill as England
captain greets
Australia's captain
Lionel Van Praag at
Wembley. Bill and
Frank Varey were
England's best pair
for England in a 63
– 44 win.

Away from the
adoring crowds, it
was down to work
on the precious
machinery in
conditions a long
way from the
clinical, operating
theatre-style
workshops enjoyed
by today's Grand
Prix stars.

Wembley had not seen *real* speedway up till then – and there had been racing there since 1929.

Elvin was somewhat startled to be informed that the Wembley track was flat and that, to put on *proper* speedway racing he would have to lower the entire sacred centre green soccer pitch three feet so that speedway riders could get some comfortable banking beneath their wheels. It was not until many years later, long after Bill Kitchen had ridden his last race for Wembley, that the middle of the stadium was indeed lowered. It was done when the football pitch was relaid. But even then, Bill used to insist, the Wembley first bend was still a flat one; there was banking only on the pit turn.

Bill Kitchen was born in Galgate, Lancashire. Even when only two, he was earning money on two wheels, performing on his mini-bike for the coach parties that stopped at the local pub. 'My grandfather was a cycle dealer,' he said. 'When cars came along he kept up with the times. It's not to be wondered at that I soon became mechanically minded.'

There was an early interest, and success, at sand racing, as a sidecar passenger and at scrambling. It led to an invitation for a trial at the Burnley speedway in 1929. 'Frank Charles was the king pin among the riders,' said Bill. I ran second in a novices' heat, but had engine trouble in the final. I got five shillings (25 pence) for my trouble and it seemed to me that it was no use trying to become a cinder rider unless you had a machine specially

built for the job. I just couldn't afford the luxury, so I forgot about the game.'

Though there was more success on the sand and grass tracks and the Isle of Man TT races, Bill said he 'had a hankering for speedway'. The Preston track was nearby and he wrote to the Scott works at Shipley asking to be loaned a machine to race there. Scotts gave him a job as a competitions rider. But, said Bill: 'There was a clause in my contract forbidding me to ride on the speedway. It was regarded as a circus and something that wouldn't last very long.'

In 1932 Bill's father happened to meet the father of Bronco Dixon, whose career took him to Middlesbrough, Sheffield, Belle Vue, Wembley and West Ham, who told him that Belle Vue boss E.O. Spence was looking for good grasstrack riders to try them out on the cinders.

Bill said: 'E.O. seemed impressed and suggested I practise at the start of the 1933 season. In every race I'd lead for several laps and then some silly engine fault would put me out. I was very upset, but E.O. wasn't. He said: "Buy a 1933 engine, Bill, and you're in the team."'

Leading the National League champions, Bill with the 1946 Wembley Lions. The picture was taken in the Belle Vue pits and the side wears their 'away' race jackets which were without the lion rampant of their 'home' colours. From the left: George Wilks, Tommy Barnet, trainer, Bob Wells, Tommy Price, Alf Bottoms, Bill, Alec Jackson, manager, Charlie May and Roy Craighead. Standing at the back Bronco Wilson.

Left: *Back at his old stamping ground in Manchester, a contrast in styles with Bill on the inside of Wally Lloyd.*

E.O was talking about his speedway team of all the talents, the classic Aces side which virtually dominated the sport throughout the Thirties – four National League titles in succession between 1933 and 1936 and the Aces were leading the table in 1939; five National Trophies in succession between 1933 and 1937; four ACU Cups in succession between 1934 and 1937 and a British Cup in 1939, plus Eric Langton pushing Wembley's Lionel Van Praag to a run-off for the 1936 World Championship.

It wouldn't be allowed today, what with points limits and all that jazz. And indeed there were many cries during that period that Belle Vue were too strong and should release riders to other teams. But E.O. Spence would have none of it. What he had he would damned well hold, he said. If other sides wanted top talent they should do what he did: go out and find it for themselves.

Belle Vue's devastating record is an indication of the quality into which the vastly inexperienced Kitchen was plunged. But, talk about an overnight sensation: within three months he had been picked as reserve for England. 'I seemed to find no difficulty in riding on cinders,' said Bill. 'My long experience on grass made sliding easy, and I was also an expert on clutch starts which were introduced in 1933. It was a wonderful season.'

One reason was his on-track partnership with the great Australian Max Grosskreutz,

The nearly man yet again. For the second year running Bill finished runner-up in the major individual event of the season, the Speedway Riders Championship Final on his home track at Wembley. In 1946 it had been team mate Tommy Price who had snatched the top prize from him, this time it was Jack Parker, who came from behind to beat him in a dramatic two-man run-off for the title. Bill Longley was third.

and he recalled it with affection. Max was a traditional leg-trailer who liked the wide open spaces near the Hyde Road boards. Bill was a newfangled foot-forward rider and he liked to tuck in close to the white line.

It was in that partnership that the seeds were sown for Bill Kitchen to become one of speedway's supreme artists. His magnificent talent was really seen at its best when he established himself as one of that elite band of great captains who, in the early post-war boom years, perfected and elevated team riding to a fine art.

And again, in the same year, Bill's challenge to Match Race Champion Vic Duggan ended in disaster and suspicion. Bill won the first leg on Duggan's home track Harringay, and Duggan is seen winning the second leg before a massive crowd at Bill's home track Wembley. A decider took place at Belle Vue, which Duggan won to keep the Golden Helmet. But the pair were summoned to a Contol Board Chamber of Justice at which the words 'fixing of a race' were used. Both men always denied the allegation and the court finally ruled that it was unable to hold either rider 'guilty of conduct prejudicial to the sport'. Following the inquiry Duggan resigned the title and declined to take part in the contest again.

The others were Norman Parker at Wimbledon, freed from the pre-war overshadowing brilliance of his brother Jack, Eric Chitty, the Canadian glamour boy crooner captain of West Ham; the immaculately flamboyant early Australian pioneer Ron Johnson at New Cross, who had also been released from the towering influence of his team mate, the 1937 World Champion Jack Milne who had stayed in America. And, to a lesser extent, the newly emerged Ron Clarke at Bradford.

It was team riding that Bill Kitchen enjoyed most about his speedway. He liked 'spreading yourself about a bit', with a less experienced partner up ahead and a wily, track-crafty, high-calibre opposition heat leader behind to outwit.

Bill did have his individual moments. There were the two World Finals of 1937 and 1938. He qualified again in 1939 and though the war prevented the meeting being held, he was in with a good chance because he was level with Wilbur Lamor-eaux of Wimbledon and the USA and team mate Eric Langton on seven bonus points, which riders in those days took with them to the Final. They all had one fewer than favourite Cordy Milne of Southampton and the USA. There was one more World Final appearance, in 1949 when he finished sixth. In each of his World Finals he scored nine points.

Sergeant Bill Kitchen of the RASC was

one of the stars in uniform who helped to keep the sport alive by continuing to race in the meetings at Belle Vue throughout the war, and later with the ENSA speedway team that toured the newly liberated Europe.

He came nearest to carrying off the top prizes in the 1946 and 1947 British Champion-ships, the major individual competitions that temporarily replaced the official World Championship, finishing second both times. In 1946 it was to his Wembley team mate Tommy Price, but Bill never forgot his breathtaking run-off with Jack Parker for the 1947 title. It had been a night of sensation because the sure-fire winner, Harringay's Australian superman Vic Duggan, who had been virtually unbeatable all season, was eclipsed by Parker in Heat 8 and then crashed out in Heat 11.

Both on 14 points, Kitchen and Parker went to the tapes for the decider. Bill had it all sewn up for most of the race because he made the gate and was being urged on by the 85,000 crowd, most of whom were his partisan Wembley fans. But it was a night when

Parker would not be denied. The majority of those who witnessed the drama saw it as a case of Jack biding his time and picking his spot before seeing his chance and exploiting it to break through to win.

Bill saw it like this: 'It was more a case of me losing it rather than Jack winning it. I locked right up and practically stopped. Jack was sufficiently close to be able to get between me and the line.'

It was, perhaps, ironic that the magazines that reported the meeting also carried the announcement of the death of the man who really launched Bill's racing career, E.O. Spence, his old boss at Belle Vue, at the age of only fifty-two.

It was about this time that Bill's talent for allowing the sport's major prizes to elude him became apparent to the speedway commentators of the day. True, in 1946 he had begun in style, winning the Newcastle Cup and the Glasgow Cup within two days of each other and then beating Tommy Price in a decider for the Easter Tourney at Belle Vue. But these were provincial baubles.

Hadn't he finished second to Price in the 1946 British Riders Championship? Hadn't he been nominated as the first post war British Match Race Champion as well, and then lost to Parker? Didn't he get another crack at it in 1947 against Duggan and lose? And here he was again, losing to Parker once more in the big 1947 Wembley Final.

There was no question, they said, of ill luck being involved in Bill Kitchen's individual near misses. His penchant for allowing the top prizes to slip from his grasp, yet be brilliant in team events, was a disability shared by many other first class speedway stars, they said.

Bill doesn't recall his final race. He thought it was almost certainly in South Africa where he rode for the Wembley Lions – who else? He was called back from his last winter tour because his mother was ill and his father suggested that it might be a good idea if he gave up racing.

But even when he was not actively leading Wembley, it didn't seem to diminish the roar of the Lions. For a while he was that rare thing in speedway, the non-riding captain. And he still found himself stepping up to receive the League Championship trophy.

For many years Bill was the official track and machine examiner at all the big events. But the British speedway bigwigs sent him a letter informing him that his services were no longer required. The implication was that they were seeking a younger man. At the time it seemed astounding that they could suddenly dispense with all that priceless experience.

They could have employed him in a different capacity. He had another talent. He could turn heads with his incredibly accurate impersonation of the sound of the two minute claxon in use at the time.

THE MAGIC OF FLASH

THIS is real speedway photographic history. It is a unique action study of Bill Kitchen, though the lion on his race jacket is not his Wembley Lion, it is the Lion of England and it was taken during a Test match in Australia.

The picture is so special because it was captured with a flash camera – which is why the action has been stopped so well. Every spoke in the wheels, every link in the chain, every visible tread in both tyres, every speck of the track surface thrown up by the back wheel and almost the blink in Bill's eyes, is in clear, sharp focus.

Pictures like this used to come from Australia regularly in the early post-war years. The Aussies were decades ahead of anyone in Europe because their track photographers were allowed to use flash when, in England at any rate, it was thought to be dangerous and they had to work with available natural light. Mike Patrick was the first to use flash on British tracks in 1985. Now, of course, it is commonplace.

Buddy Fuller

THE RUFFIAN INVADER

THE NUMBER of lines devoted to Buddy Fuller in the seminal speedway booklet *Who's Who In Speedway 1949* is 18 – fewer than Jock Grierson and Ron Clark and the same number as Ken Tidbury, all Buddy's Hastings team mates that season.

But as a certain venerable football team manager is oft quoted as having said when comparing his sport to the matters of life and death, Buddy Fuller was '*much more important than that*'.

Buddy blows in: Proudly displaying the Hastings colours in 1948.

Arthur John 'Buddy' Fuller invaded the British speedway scene from his native South Africa at Third Division Hastings in 1948. And just like that other Hastings invasion by the Normans more than 800 years before, Buddy made a conquest in a very short time.

His arrival was reported like this: 'There was the day in mid-season when Buddy Fuller blew in. Buddy was just a guy from South Africa over here for a holiday and taking soundings as to whether any English riders would like a trip to South Africa during the winter.

'Buddy had ridden a bit in the Union and, apart from his holiday, he wondered whether he could get a ride or two over here. Buddy was around when Hastings's Wally Green and one or two others were on the injured list, and chief Charlie Dugard took a chance and signed the South African to get himself out of a hole.

'Well, at his first Hastings meeting Buddy ran out with 10 points, followed it with four at awkward Exeter, seven at stiff Southampton and then got 11 against Coventry. Needless to say, Mr Fuller was a regular for as long as he cared to stay.'

Those words came from the author of *Who's Who In Speedway 1949*, the highly experienced and greatly respected journalist Tom Broadsider Morgan of *The People* newspaper.

With 42 points against his name there was an early return to his homeland for Buddy, but he was back in 1949 in even better form. Then disaster struck him and Hastings.

In mid season a court injunction against noise was upheld and Hastings were ordered to cease racing by October. At the same time, Buddy had a really bad crash and his skull was fractured.

He remembered the incident like this: 'On 27 July 1949 I won my first three rides at Hastings's and was leading on my way to my first full maximum, when I overslid and fell only to be struck by a following rider. I suffered a fractured skull and was paralysed on the right side of my face.

'My crash brought to light a ruse I had been using. In South Africa we didn't wear gloves when racing, but this was compulsory in British speedway … I wore a glove on my left hand and painted my right (*his throttle hand*) hand black.'

Buddy's Hastings team mate at the time, Ken Middleditch, who was to go on to find fame and enjoy a distinguished career with Poole and Swindon, said: 'It was remarkable how he recovered especially as he was paralysed down one side of his face.'

Though there was a riding comeback of sorts with Liverpool in 1950, Buddy struggled. And, discouraged by his lack of success, he once more returned home. But he had opened the door to British speedway for his fellow South Africans, such as Doug Serrurier, one of five racing brothers, and Fred Wills at Liverpool. To follow were Fred Lang at Wembley,

The early entrepreneur, Buddy with his South African team and the visiting 1948-1949 England touring side. Wearing their Union Jacks are, from left, Ted Gibson, Jimmy Dunn, Wilf Plant, Jeff Bishop, Ken Tidbury and Ken Middleditch. Buddy is second from left in the middle row, behind him Doug Serrurier, Harry Du Toit, Oska Wessman. Kneeling Fred Wills, Joe Blankfield, Toby Boshoff.

Roy Bester at Leicester and Neil Mortimer and Arthur Duncan at Birmingham.

The outstanding Henry Long was already making his mark at Belle Vue and Doug Davies was to do the same at Birmingham, both of whom were to go on to qualify for World Finals.

Buddy said: 'I must say that I enjoyed racing in Britain. All I had to do was take my bike to the meeting and ride. Whereas in South Africa I was designing and constructing tracks – nine alone while I was an active speedway rider. I was also riding and promoting.

'This meant that I had to see to the organisation of the meeting, the publicity, programmes, public address, catering, insurance and methanol for the bikes as well as riding.'

The Fuller motorcycling legend had begun almost

Looks as though it has been a really hard meeting for Jock Grierson, Ken Middledtich and Buddy.

twenty years earlier in the mid-Thirties. Of those early days he recalled: 'I am perhaps better known as a speedway rider, but in an active racing career that spanned from 1935 to 1970 it included road racing, speedway, stock cars and sprint car racing.'

If the major international prizes were to elude him on the track, his subsequent exploits as a promoter of motor sports earned him numerous titles in his native land. A few were: Mr Speedway, Mr Cinders, Mr Stock Car Racing and Mr Hot Rods.

'One of my first memorable races was at Waverley in Pretoria in 1942,' said Buddy. 'My main opponent was a road racer. We were both riding Nortons and the circuit we were riding on had a dirt surface. This was where my speedway experience came to my advantage because I did not have to brake on the short corners, while he was breaking heavily.'

Then, as now perhaps, speedway riders were not the most fashionable of sportsmen, but they could pull in the paying customers. Buddy remembered that once he had a call inviting speedway riders to take part in a special hill climb. He said: 'The promoter told me: "We want you ruffians along to bring in the crowds." Well, we ruffians arrived and so did the crowds.'

He started riding dirt track speedway in 1938, winning the South African championship the following year and again in 1946. The war had disrupted South African speedway as it had elsewhere, and there was no contest in 1947.

The determined display that won Buddy Fuller his chance when he 'invaded' the British speedway scene looking for a ride or two.

It was revived in 1948 and, said Buddy, he badly wanted to win it so that he could claim he had held the title for ten years, though it was only the third South African championship to be staged during that period. He did win, dropping his only point to Fred Wills and beating Henry Long on the way.

He formed, and became chairman of, the South African Speedway Riders Association. And it is undoubtedly largely due to him that, in the heady days of the 1950s, South Africa became the preferred winter destination instead of Australia for many of the top names in British speedway.

Barry and June Briggs chose South Africa for their honeymoon, so did Peter and Brenda Craven and Fred and Pat Williams.

Buddy not only organised, welcomed, looked after and guided visiting international speedway teams to his country, he also took teams overseas to spread the South African gospel abroad.

Five times World Champion Ove Fundin raced in South Africa for Buddy, and long after Buddy had retired from racing and was living in a retirement home, Ove went to visit him. He recalls: 'There was nothing wrong with Buddy's mental health, he knew me straight away and we talked for hours, a lot of it about a tour Buddy made with a team of South African riders in Sweden. It was easy to tell what a strong man Buddy was in his prime and that he was a real gentleman. His son was an airline captain with South African Airways and he once brought Buddy to England where he was guest of honour at the old Veteran Speedway Riders Association annual dinner.'

Reg Duval, Buddy's team mate at Liverpool, says: 'Buddy not only arranged for teams to visit South Africa but he also arranged for the visiting riders to take out spares and parts and then he re-sold them to the local riders. He was very much an entrepreneur.

'He and Trevor Redmond were going into partnership but they fell out and Buddy went ahead on his own. But Trevor managed to get Buddy and his tracks blacklisted. Most of the Birmingham riders were out there at the time and, because they were deemed to be riding on illegal tracks, they were banned when they returned to England. Which led to Birmingham closing just after the start of the 1957 British season.

'Buddy went into staging car meetings, but then in 1961 he asked me, as I was out there, if I would help him restart speedway so I stayed on for about six weeks. Then someone informed the authorities that Buddy was staging speedway again and once more he and all his riders, including me, were banned. But this time the British speedway authorities did nothing about it.'

Fred Williams, World Champion in 1950 and 1953, also made the close season trip to South Africa. Fred said: 'Buddy was very thankful to me because I had arranged with him in the August of 1953 to go out there and race while on honeymoon. Well, it just so

Left: *Taking soundings: Buddy in his business suit and his role as roving ambassador for South African speedway at Custom House with West Ham stars Aub Lawson (left) and Tommy Croombs.*
Right: *Spreading the gospel: Buddy at the head of the 1951 South African team setting off for an overseas tour. Standing from left: Toby Boshof, Alec Bankfield, Harry du Toit, Bob Raw, Buddy on bike. Kneeling, from left: Maurice Fenton, Joe Blankfield.*

happened that I won the World Championship that year. And Buddy rang me up, sounding very worried. He asked me if I was still coming. "Yes", I said. "And will the terms still be the same?" he said. I said: "Yes of course".

'So it was arranged for Pat and I to fly out there ahead of the rest of the team who were going by boat. I'd arranged for my bike to be sent – because in those days we had only one bike. Not like it is today.

'Buddy organised a practice session at Wembley Stadium in Johannesburg and he said to me: "Well, let's see you do a few laps, because the first thing I want you to do is have a match race with Henry Long who is our best rider here in South Africa."

'My bike had been tuned at Wembley by Cyril Spinks, who wasn't a mechanic who experimented. All our bikes at Wembley were absolutely standard JAPs. So off I went, and when I came in Buddy said: "Is that the best you can do? You're just not going fast enough. There is no way I can put you against Henry Long. I think what we'd better do is put one of my engines in your bike. So he and I switched my Wembley JAP for one of his.

'I went so much better after that and did beat Henry. Because of the altitude there – about 7,000ft or 8,000ft, the bikes performed differently and that's why I had seemed so slow.

'Buddy also ran a track at Durban which was about 400 miles away from Johannesburg where the meetings were on a Saturday night. The Durban meetings were on Sunday afternoons.

'Buddy had bought a huge Bedford lorry. The front was fitted out with bunk beds for the riders and at the back there was room for about 15 speedway bikes. We would set off after the Saturday meeting to drive through the night for the following day's meeting at Durban.

'Because of the insurance only three drivers were allowed. Dick Campbell was one, then there was me and Buddy. Howdy Byford was my co-driver. We always made it on time, even though the lorry had a top speed of only about 60mph. The roads were really just dirt tracks – they hadn't been made up then.

'There were quite a lot of hills and by putting the lorry into neutral and coasting down the hills we could get up to about 90 mph, passing astonished car drivers as we went. We had some hilarious times.

Great times, remembered by the teams of British stars who raced in South Africa on Buddy's tours. From left: Fred Williams, Don Perry, Bill Kitchen, Ian Williams, Brian Crutcher, Reg Duval, Bob Griffiths, Howdy Byford and Buddy.

Buddy liked to put on a show and here he has arranged a massed line-up of speedway riders on less than potent machinery. And they seem to be enjoying it maybe even more than the crowd.

Recalling old times at a Veteran Speedway Riders Association annual dinner in England: Buddy, centre, Fred Williams, left, and former VSRA President Danny Dunton.

'But there was that trouble between Buddy and Trevor Redmond and it was then that the Birmingham riders were banned.'

One of them was Eric Boothroyd, then one of Birmingham's top stars. Eric says: 'Buddy was Mr South African Speedway and up to that time Trevor Redmond and Buddy were mates. But there was a falling out.'

The incident became known as the South African Farce. It was announced that all members of the British touring party would be fined and banned. They included Birmingham's top three, Alan Hunt, Ron Mountford and Eric Boothroyd. Hunt was involved in a fatal accident before he returned to Britain and with the banning of the others, Birmingham promoter Les Marshall was faced with a decimated team.

Eric says that there was a confrontation with British Control Board manager Major Bill Fearnley, described by Eric as 'a bit of a terror', who told Marshall: 'Listen, old boy, your riders are banned.' So Marshall said: 'If that's the way you're going to treat us after all we've done for speedway, I'll close Birmingham down.' And he did.

'But Buddy Fuller was a great bloke,' insists Eric. 'It was a difficult situation, but he paid us, and got us and our kids tickets back home.'

'Buddy was a lovely person,' says Ken Middlditch: 'I spent several seasons in South Africa. The money wasn't fantastic but you didn't have to break your neck racing. Everything Buddy promised he delivered. I lived with his family on one trip and we had a wonderful time. He really looked after the English boys.

'He was great for South African speedway, but he did have trouble with Trevor Redmond who tried to take over.'

Brian Crutcher, who as a nineteen-year-old enjoyed a superlative 1953-54 South African season, dropping a mere three points in four Tests, says: 'Buddy was always asking us to put on a show to make the racing look good.'

But there was a time when Brian resorted to drastic action because for once Buddy declined to pay up. Brian says: 'The car being used by Don Perry and me caught fire and Buddy refused to pay for a replacement. So I parked my bike across the start line at one meeting and wouldn't remove it until we were paid. Buddy did pay us in the end and we bought another car.

'But they were great times.'

Great times indeed, especially for Buddy Fuller, who died on 9 May, 2005 aged eighty-nine. He once remarked of his career in the saddle: 'Speedway teams were knights of the oval track. I suppose I must have had several hundred girls after me in those days.'

ARTHUR JOHN "BUDDY" FULLER

Tomasz Gollob

A PASSION FOR THE PAST AND HOPE FOR THE FUTURE

THE legendary names we have chosen to include in this volume have all left the speedway scene. They are either not actively riding any more or they are dead. We wanted to include one real living racing legend – and we can claim a unique journalistic capture with this very rare interview with the magnificent, the controversial Tomasz Gollob, Poland's most outstanding, most idolised and most highly paid sporting personality of the modern era. The world of speedway acknowledges that Gollob is not only a superb speedway rider, he is a brilliant, highly skilled motorcyclist, a track star of exceptional talent and stature.

In 2007 Gollob and fellow rider Rune Holta survived a plane crash on their way to a speedway meeting at Tarnów. The aircraft was being flown by Tomasz's father Władysław. Gollob escaped with cuts and bruises after pulling his father from the wreckage.

Tomasz doesn't give interviews – not usually and never easily. But in this endeavour we have been fortunate to have the assistance of our friend, the distinguished Polish journalist Tomasz Lorek* who was trusted by Gollob enough for him to finally agree, after some time, to talk frankly about his life and career especially for our book of *Speedway Legends*. What follows is Tomasz Lorek's excellent translation from his native Polish. Lorek writes:

No doubt he was born with a God-given natural talent to race motorcycles. Some people think he had a bike in his cradle. That he is a genius who doesn't like to compromise, always has his own way of thinking. It is the philosophy of a perfectionist. Now, Tomasz has matured, he was 44 this year, older and wiser, he puts things into a wider perspective. When he met me he was punctual. He was very nice, easy to talk to, very open. He was wearing pyjamas in his bed after a practise in a gym late evening, close to midnight. You could hear the hounds of winter, like in the popular song composed by Sting in his album Mercury Falling. Snow behind the trees sunken in a cold weather. Our conversation was truly out of the world of ghosts. Tomasz Gollob is from the old school of speedway, he likes to walk via spiritual avenues. But he answered all the questions plus one from me.

Tomasz, how did you fall in love with speedway? What first gave you an interest in speedway?

As a very small kid I loved sport in general. I was dreaming to be a professional athlete. No matter what discipline, if it was football or ice hockey. I played a lot of football for fun

The inspiration: Tomasz and Papa Władysław.

when I was a kid. My father Władysław is responsible for my huge love for riding a motorcycle. He was so happy to see me on a bike. My father raced on bikes, he was very interesting and knowledgeable in engineering and racing. When I was a boy, I managed to learn how to ride a bike. I raced motocross, I did some road racing, I tried rallies, enduro. Speedway was a final destination, I tried different types of motorcycling, then I switched to speedway.

That's where train terminates, the very last railway station of your wonderful journey.
True. Speedway seemed to be my place, a station I get off and I feel so great about it.

Has there been a hero, someone who you have modelled yourself on?
Yes, of course. Anton 'Toni' Mang, he was a road racer from West Germany. I can't precisely tell you how old I was when I first saw him in action: maybe eight, possibly nine years old. He was bloody good on 250 cc and 350 cc bikes. He was racing on a green Kawasaki. He was a World Champion in road racing, 250 cc engine capacity in 1980, 1981 and 1987. He was also a World Champion in 350 cc in 1981 and 1982. Actually he was a last 350 cc World Champion as the class was abolished at the end of the 1982. I truly admired him.

From road racing into a sport of a shale ... Why did you decide to ride in Britain for Ipswich Witches?
I always wanted to be a World Champion in speedway. I decided to see how I would cope with different type of speedway tracks. I wanted to experience British tracks, be more flexible on the bike, I wanted to be smooth while racing a speedway bike and I was interested to see different culture of speedway racing. My good friend and a fellow countrywoman, Magda Louis, was a promoter in Ipswich those days. She offered me a place in a team and I raced there from 1998 until 2000. I signed for three years, but I had a very serious accident in 1999 just a few days before a final Grand Prix round in Vojens. That accident convinced me to cut my racing schedule. I clearly saw I had too many racing commitments and my body needed a bit of a rest. Those years I had around 120, 130 meetings. That's an enormous amount of racing. To be perfectly honest, it's a dose that can kill you as a human being. But there's no doubt racing in England has helped me a lot

Showing off all the natural talent: Tomasz displays the superb balance of the perfectionist.

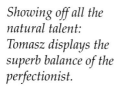

The survivors: They might have cheated death in a plane crash, but when it came to the racetrack it was every man for himself and Tomasz decides to get heavy with Rune Holta.

to improve my skills and broaden horizons. It's a true saying that England is a very good school of racing for young riders.

Have you ever thought that you should stay longer in England?

No, no, I didn't want to race there for few more seasons, because it's a huge challenge. Racing in England is so demanding, you have to be energetic all the time. You need plenty of preparations to be ready to race in UK. Travelling twice a week to England was a huge task. I spent three years in England and I believed it was enough for me to get another experience. I simply understood that it was too much. Don't forget I was also racing in Sweden, sometimes in Denmark, plus regular racing in Poland, so for the majority of my career I was competing in three or even four leagues in Europe. It's a lot of effort.

Yes, you also raced for Fredericia Motor Klub in Denmark at the beginning of your career on international stage.

Yes, that's true. 1994 until 1996. I had to cut my racing schedule, because it was simply impossible to score well with the big amount of contracted meetings. But I want to admit that England and racing abroad helped me to become a world class rider.

What answer do you have for people who criticized you for an aggressive style of racing. These people think that sometimes you pushed too hard or even exaggerate. You were so dynamic on a bike, so hungry to win every single race … Do you agree you were sometimes too aggressive with on-track manoeuvres?

Yes, I agree … I was young, I was ambitious, I was aggressive on a speedway track. It was toe to toe and shoulder to shoulder, you can say it was a close racing, in contact, but also it was a fair racing. I didn't harm any rider, I didn't cause other rider to fall on a track. It's obvious a young rider doesn't have a feeling of a magic touch on a throttle. A young rider is not responsible when he comes to the tapes or fights in a tight first corner bunching. It's pretty normal that an attack or a courageous move made by an inexperienced young fellow is far away from being well-balanced. Experience comes with an age.

Did you ever wish you hadn't had to compete with Tony Rickardsson for the World Championship and what do you think of Tony?

I have never regretted that I had to compete with Tony Rickardsson for the World Championship crown. Before my rivalry with Tony, I had to compete with Hans Nielsen, Tommy Knudsen, Jimmy Nilsen and many other world class riders. Then there was a time when my main rival was Tony Rickardsson. No doubt Tony was my major competitor. It looked like there was a huge opportunity for me to collect World Championship titles, but Tony was a fantastic speedway rider and a great rival. There's no doubt Tony made speedway a very popular sport in Sweden. He was a major obstacle I can't come through … I am pretty sure Tony can confirm it, that he was a great rider, but for some reason he was so consistent and he was also able to use his chances when I was injured. But even when I was healthy and in a top shape, he was so quick and adapted so fast to changing track conditions, so he proved his class. Tony was a marvelous rider, he deserved to be a six times World Champion. He was a champ because of his greatness, not because someone had an engine failure or got excluded or touched the tapes. He was out of this world, a

The team mates: Gollob and Tony Rickardsson in the hugely successful Ipswich side of 1998 which swept the honours board, winning the League Championship, the Craven Shield and the Knock Out Cup. The line-up is, from the left, Tomasz, Tony Svab, Tony Rickardsson, Chris Louis, Savalas Clouting and Scott Nicholls.

Controversy … Tomasz's aggressive racing tactics sometimes resulted in retribution and he ended up face down at the 1995 Hackney Grand Prix after a punch from irate Australian Craig Boyce, who decided it was payback time after being brought down in a crunch clash between the pair.

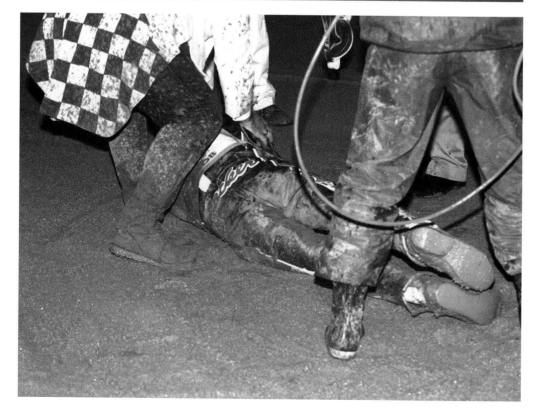

Another post race encounter with America's Billy Hamill at the German Grand Prix in the Pocking pits … with Tomasz being restrained and bikes having been abandoned in the scuffle.

highly talented speedway rider. He is a true legend of Swedish and international speedway. It's not a one night wonder, he was born to be an excellent speedway rider. A world class rider.

How did you cope with being Poland's top athlete and what are pros and cons of being a person so recognizable even for people outside of speedway society?
I am extremely happy and glad to be recognizable among Polish sportsmen. A fame doesn't disturb me at all. I feel I am still a normal person. I didn't change because I am a famous speedway rider and a former World Champion. Honestly, I think I am the same as when I was a boy who was pretty unknown to the world. Being an icon or a World

Chasing four-times World Champion Hans Nielsen of Denmark who Tomasz considers one of the 'true legends'. But not forgetting how much he admires England's Mark Loran who is right behind at Coventry.

Champion doesn't give you a right to walk on clouds. I still like to touch a pavement by my feet and I prefer to stay normal. Of course, a fame can turn you into negatives, but as long as I stay a normal man, I can't see any negatives. It obviously has its positives. A very positive thing is that people from my country look at me as a World Champion, a legend and a part of a history of a Polish sport.

You raced for more than two decades on a speedway bike. Are there any riders you dislike and are there any riders you respect them so much?
I don't know any rider I dislike. I like all the riders, I understand the passion they have to compete in such an extreme sport like speedway. I am so lucky that I had a chance to compete against true legends: Hans Nielsen was one of them. For sure Tony Rickardsson is a rider I admire a lot and I also have a huge amount of respect for an Aussie icon Jason Crump. Another fantastic rider I will always admire is Leigh Adams, a phenomenal rider with a fabulous style of racing. Well, I competed with so many riders, I also can't forget fierce battles I had against Polish riders. I mean, I competed on a very high level with Polish riders who were or still are a big part of Grands Prix series. I had a lot of sympathy for their efforts and I admire them for all the hard work they do to be able to compete on a top flight level of speedway.

Being in your armchair, I would definitely add a rider who always was fair on track, 2000 World Champion, a great British rider, Mark Loram.
Oh, yes, Mark definitely is among riders I admire the most. I am sorry if anyone feels that I forgot about him. It's natural I can't mention all the riders but those who I didn't mention I don't want them to think that I don't remember them. I respect every single rider from an old school, the generation of riders I had a privilege to compete with them. They were great riders and I had a lot of sympathy for them.

You survived a plane crash – what effect did it have on your attitude to life? Do you have a slightly different approach to a life after you managed to stay alive through a big disaster?

Looking for Tomasz … the magnificent six-times World title winner Tony Rickardsson of Sweden is cool enough to keep Tomasz in his place while dealing with the inside challenge of 'Aussie icon' Jason Crump at the same time.

A plane crash hasn't changed me at all. I look on many aspects of a life exactly the same as before I had this horrendous crash. I had plenty of accidents. I was seriously injured on speedway track, I had car accidents, I survived an aircraft crash, I got injured on a push bike, on a boat. All these accidents has no influence on how I see the world, the philosophy of life. Accidents didn't change the way I stare at speedway, my activities or the way I prepare to race on a bike with no brakes. Now, when I get older, I sometimes surprise myself that I could have come through. Sometimes I ask myself how did I manage to come over all these obstacles and maintain a top form. I can hardly believe how I was able to survive and fight against all the bad luck I had almost every single year during my speedway career.

Indeed, it's a fascinating story of what a man can do in tough circumstances if he has an aim and a mental strength. Tomasz, why is Polish speedway the best in the world and why Polish riders are so successful?
Polish speedway was, is and will be in a top shape, because Polish people love this discipline. It's about emotions and a passion for a sport. We've got the most beautiful speedway stadiums in the world. We've got the most professional league racing. Poland managed to attract top riders in the world. There's definitely the strongest riders field in Polish league. All other European leagues can't compete with Polish league racing, because passion, equipment, excitement and level of racing is the highest in Poland.

Is speedway going to be different within next ten, twenty years? A huge progress in technology or efforts to simplify the sport will make a huge impact on speedway?
I think it all depends on people from governing body and promoters. If the people who run the clubs will be sensible, if they will have a right strategy to help speedway become a bigger sport, if they will take care about riders' safety, then I am happy to see a bright future for speedway. I can only hope there will not be crazy decisions about silencers. Someone has to open eyes and see how many riders got injured 'thanks' to modern silencers. Speedway will increase its popularity if people from governing bodies will make wise decisions. If someone will bring irrational decisions, then speedway may be in trouble. For now, I can't see any major obstacles or problems with speedway. All that's happening with speedway is very positive, like geographical exposure via Aussie Grand Prix in Melbourne and wide television coverage thanks to Speed-way Grand Prix and Speedway European Championship.

What other career would you have if not on the speedway track?
For sure I would spend my life within the sport family, because I love sport and I love to

A champagne moment for three: Tony Rickardsson wins his second successive World Championship at Vojens in 1999 with Tomasz second – one place better than the previous year – and Hans Nielsen third.

World Champion at last: The other six-times World Champion Ivan Mauger makes the presentation at the official FIM ceremony in 2010 when Tomasz receives his gold medal and citation.

compete. I remember my father wanted me to become a lawyer or a doctor. I decided to be a professional sportsman. If I hadn't been a speedway rider, I would definitely turn to motocross. If I hadn't been a motocross rider, I would become a footballer.

How about Moto GP or World Superbikes?
I raced motocross, I did a lot of road racing. It was a pure pleasure. I love all the motorcycling disciplines.

What are you planning to do when you retire from racing?
I fulfilled my dreams. I was always dreaming about being a World Champion in speedway and I managed to do it in 2010. I had a wonderful time on a bike, but I didn't say a last word. I still give myself a few more years to race speedway and a bit of a motocross. After I retire, I will be open to answer any questions from young people who will try to learn a tough trade of speedway. I will help young guns to come through the tough times in speedway, tell them what to do to be happy on a speedway bike. For sure I will stay close to the sport of speedway. I will try not to disturb, I will take a look from a different perspective, I will do everything to help speedway become a bigger and a better sport. I really care about this sport and I want speedway to develop in a right direction.

Tomasz Gollob was Speedway World Champion in 2010. His other titles include being Polish national champion eight times, there have been five World Cup victories and he was made Poland's Sports Personality Of The Year in 1999. For his sporting achievements, the Order Of Polonia Restitute awarded him the Knight's Cross (5th Class) in 2000, the Officer's Cross (4th Class) in 2007 and the Commander's Cross in 2010.

Ever the showman: Acknowledging the acclaim of fans at his home town Grand Prix in Bydgoszcz.

*Tomasz Lorek is a freelance writer from Wroclaw. He is a television commentator and reporter covering motorsports (speedway, freestyle motocross, F1) and tennis. A correspondent of **Speedway Star** *and* Tygodnik Zuzlowy, *he writes for various newspapers and magazines, is a centre green announcer at speedway events, and works for Polsat Sport, Poland's major sports television channel.*

Alan Hunt

WHACKER!

WHACKER HUNT idolised Birmingham. And Birmingham idolised Whacker Hunt. It was a mutual admiration society that lasted throughout the decade of his speedway career until being tragically, cruelly and prematurely ended almost six decades ago now.

Although, come to think about it, it really continues to this day among those who had the great good fortune to witness the magic of Alan 'Whacker' Hunt in action. Perchance even among those who were not yet born when he thrilled the cheering crowds every week, from the black hills of Cradley Heath to speedway's glittering early post-war Mecca, London, its great fashionable arenas … and beyond.

In the words of a speedway commentator far more distinguished than I, 'the memory of Alan Hunt is still as big and wide as his grin. He had something in common with all the most notable speedway greats – he was a personality. He was a colourful character and, at the time of his tragic passing, he was rated among the dozen top men in his profession.'

Whacker is one of speedway's immortals who lost his life in a racing crash. It happened in South Africa and he had risen to eminence, excellence and fame the hard way. When the Alan Hunt whirlwind first hit the cinder tracks of the Midlands, one promoter begged for him to be banned before other riders who had the misfortune to find themselves on the same track with him came to serious harm. But watching the polished performer Whacker became in later years was to experience true speedway artistry.

As Petty-Officer Hunt of His Majesty's Royal Navy he had his application to be a post-war Special Services frogman rejected. He lacked one vital aptitude: he was unable to swim. So he was discharged into an unsuspecting Birmingham Civvy Street. He hadn't been long in it when a pal asked him if he fancied going to the speedway at Perry Barr.

The invitation prompted the infamous Hunt remark: 'Speedway? What's speedway?' But he went – and was not impressed. Then, at the end of the season, they asked for volunteers to be taught how to be speedway riders. Able to resist anything but temptation, Alan applied … and was accepted.

He was trainee No.45 and a real speedway innocent. It didn't help when, at the first practice session, a fellow trainee crashed and was killed. When it came to his turn to show what he could do, he couldn't fall off. No.45 broke all the speedway rules and got away with it. Given a second half booking at Birmingham, he wasn't due out until Heat 19, but he warmed up his machine after every race on the programme. Alan made sure he had a 'hot' bike when his turn came.

Second Division Birmingham had a nursery track in the brand new Third Division at Cradley Heath, and Alan was sent there for the 1947 season. It was another Hunt classic: 'Cradley? Where's Cradley?' he inquired.

At Dudley Wood he began to make frequent and painful acquaintance with the pit bend safety fence. Alan whacked it so often it became known as Whacker's Bit – and that's how he got the unique handle to his name.

He started his racing career at the very bottom – as a Third Division reserve, lucky if he managed to score a point or two. There was only one way for

About to 'Ommer Um' … the original Cradley Heathens of 1947. Standing from left: Eric Irons, Les Beaumont, Frank Buck manager, Les Marshall promoter, Ray Beaumont, Geoff Bennett, Bob Fletcher. Sitting: Alan Hunt, Jimmy Wright, Phil Malpass.

Late starters ... the Heathens march out on opening night at Dudley Wood, Saturday June 21, 1947 with the Beaumont brothers, Ray and Les, leading followed by Alan Hunt, Phil Malpass, Eric Irons, Geoff Bennett, Stan Crouch and Jimmy Wright. Cradley beat Wombwell 46 – 36 in a Division Three league match. Alan scored 3 points.

Whacker all dolled up on the day he and Eve were married. Their guard of honour from the left are: Roy Moreton, Bill Clifton, Ray Beaumont, Les Beaumont, the groom and bride, Jimmy Wright, Phil Malpass and Eric Irons.

The polished performer, Alan on the inside of Peter Lansdale of Walthamstow.

Left: *Jokers wild, Dick Bradley, Split Waterman and Alan clown for the camera before a Test match at Wembley.*

Right: *In the colours of his beloved Birmingham, all the dynamism and fiery temperament of Alan Hunt is captured in this unique racing image. It put Whacker alongside the world's best.*

Whacker Hunt to go. That was up, and from this chaotic beginning there emerged what came to be recognised as a rare and precious talent.

Progress was at first unpredictable, but his pairing with Cradley team mate Eric Irons eventually became the scourge of Division Three – Eric with his truly brilliant team-riding, and Alan with his speed and daredevilry which, on numerous occasions, amounted to wildness. But he was learning, and on his way. Though one writer described him thus: 'Hunt at times was something of an enigma. Some of his erratic form was due to his smashing two frames within a week … '. Whacker was only consolidating his reputation.

A measure of the Hunt climb to prominence came in 1949. Cradley moved up to the Second Division and Alan took it in his stride, ending the season ranked third in the league with only Bristol's Billy Hole and Ashfield's Ken 'White Ghost' LeBreton above him – though he scored more points than LeBreton. By the following year he was a full international, becoming the first Second Division rider post-war to ride for England in a senior Test and making his debut against Australia at New Cross.

At the time, riding for England was the summit of his career ambition. It made Whacker the hottest English prospect around and the big time began to beckon, principally from London glamour club Harringay. The Racers went public on Friday May 26, announcing that they had signed Alan for a record £2,500 and he would ride for them against Wimbledon that night.

It was the transfer that never was and became a speedway *cause celebre* when Alan not only did not ride for Harringay that night, but apparently disappeared completely. Birmingham boss Les Marshall stepped in and upped the ante by offering £3,000 for his services. Cradley were furious. Marshall had snatched future international star Blond Bombshell Graham Warren from them in 1948. Little more than a couple of years later he took Alan as well.

Alan took off – literally – in this first bend incident at Perry Barr in a match against New Cross. Bob Roger fell in front of Alan who was launched into space when he ski-jumped off Roger's back wheel. Eric Boothroyd and Eric French sweep past on the inside.

The summit of Alan's ambition – riding for England. It was more important than money … and this is it: Alan is in third place at Wimbledon behind Australians Jack Biggs and his Birmingham team mare Arthur Payne with Fred Williams at the back.

Captain Dynamic: Alan, on the bike, with the 1953 Birmingham team. From left Phil Malpass, Ron Mountford, Bill Jemison, Ron Barrett, Lionel Watling, Ron Mason, Arthur Payne, Graham Warren, Phil 'Tiger' Hart, manager and Eric Boothroyd.

Actually Marshall only snatched them back – they were his riders in the first place. He believed in encouraging youth and spent very little buying in talent.

Eve, Alan's widow, explained it to me like this: 'Alan was very ambitious. Riding for England was, to him, more important than money and he saw Harringay as the door to the top flight First Division experience he needed to ride regularly for England.

'But,' she said, 'basically Alan was a Brummie through and through and he really wanted to ride for Birmingham. At Cradley they thought the sun shone out of Alan's backside and for him to go to Birmingham, just across the Black Country, was like killing the king.'

After all the furore had died down, Alan did go to Birmingham, sacrificing his share of any transfer money. At the time, Marshall owned Birmingham and Cradley and therefore Alan's contract. So there was no percentage of the transfer fee when Alan finally went to Perry Barr. Marshall got an official rap over the knuckles for how he had handled the situation – but he'd got his man. And Alan was where he really wanted to be.

The Hunt contribution to the Brummies was dynamic. He made the step up to First Division, and world class, so well that at the end of the 1951 season only West Ham's Aub Lawson had scored more league points. Whacker scored better than such major international stars as Jack Parker at Belle Vue, Split Waterman at Harringay, Fred Williams and Tommy Price at Wembley and Norman Parker and Ronnie Moore at Wimbledon. He rode in four of that year's five Tests against Australia and reached the first of his four World Finals.

The fiery Hunt temperament was not dimmed by the company he was now keeping. There were heat-of-the-moment on-track clashes with Sweden's Ove Fundin, and during one Wembley Test against the Swedes an infamous high speed altercation with Olle Nygren which made the Carter-Penhall incident at Los Angeles in the 1982 World Final seem like a slapstick custard pie fight.

In 1956, his finest season, he captained his country at last. Alan always said: 'The greatest honour a man can have in this game is riding for England. It beats all the Match Race and World Championships too'. The philosophy could explain why his Wembley World Final showings between 1951 and 1956 were mediocre, to say the least – the highest he finished was 11th.

But he had shouldered the responsibility of being Birmingham's number one, had reached the very top of his profession in what was then, truly, the world's best and toughest speedway league, and he was as lionised at Birmingham as he had been at Cradley. That year Alan outscored even the great Ove Fundin in the league, only Brian Crutcher, Barry Briggs and Ronnie Moore had better points totals.

In the British close season the Hunts took to wintering in South Africa and they were so taken with the place it became known they would settle there eventually. The South African speedway authorities decided that this made Alan eligible to ride for South Africa and,

Above left: Proudly wearing the distinctive Lion race jacket of England, Alan, left and paired with Tommy Price, adjusts his goggles as manager Fred Evans offers strategic advice. Split Waterman looks on and the white helmet cover of Graham Warren can just be seen in the back ground.

Above right: Alan takes his place among the England superstars. Standing at the back from left: Fred Williams, Ronnie Greene manager, Cyril Brine, Eddie Rigg. Seated: Norman Parker, Cyril Roger, Jack Parker, Split Waterman and Whacker.

The hand of experience … Alan offers some detail on technique to a youthful Arthur Forrest of Bradford.

Adoring autograph hunting fans – mostly female – surround their hero with team mate Wilf Willstead helping out.

True speedway artistry: Eve Hunt claimed Alan was not 'a stylish rider', but this is Hunt at his best, relaxed and full of confidence

sensationally, included him in their side for the second Test against a Scandinavian touring team.

Super patriot Alan astounded his English fans by throwing in his lot with the Springboks. The South African national championship followed – but, strangely, Alan began to have motor problems in Pretoria and became convinced that some mysterious force had started to act against him …

On 1 February, 1957, at Wembley Stadium, Johannesburg, riding for Durban Hornets against Klerksdorp Hawks, came the fatal accident. Alan was leading the race for his third win of the night when his motor stopped. He high-sided and was struck by a following rider, dying from his injuries in the early hours of the following morning. He was cremated and Eve took him back home to England.

She said: 'Alan wasn't a styish rider – it was all s**t or bust with him. He couldn't tune a bike. He tried but he was hopeless. He just liked riding for Birmingham, that was the top and bottom of it. He was a nice man who put his principles before money. He loved racing against good riders like Peter Craven and Jack Young. Like them, he was fair, square and true, but if anyone was rotten to him on the track, he always got his own back – and he made no bones about it.'

In a poignant postscript to the tragedy, Alan faced posthumous suspension, along with some of his Birmingham team mates, because they had ridden on unlicensed tracks, according to the South African Speedway Control Board. The row followed them all back to England and, in the end, their ban resulted in Les Marshal pulling the plug at Perry Barr.

Not only was Alan, the man who loved and lived for speedway, gone, but his beloved Brummies went with him.

The bikes were not to be heard again regularly at the old Alexander Sports Stadium, Perry Barr, for another half a century. When they were, the first meeting was for the Alan Hunt Memorial Trophy.

John Chaplin saw his first speedway at Perry Barr, Birmingham in 1946 and is, unashamedly, a lifelong Birmingham fan.

Wilbur Lamoreaux
THE QUIET AMERICAN

H E WAS the personification of speedway elegance. He radiated class and possessed an economy of style that was at once immaculate, dazzling and deadly.

He perfected the classic tactical racing manoeuvre of teasing an opponent with a glimpse of his front wheel on the outside, then switching his attack lightning-like to arrow past on the inside. .

It was so devastatingly successful that it became universally known as The Lammy. It is known as the 'Cut Back' to modern fans.

Such sparkling, clinical precision on the track was in sharp contrast to his off-track personality.

He was a pocket dynamo. One of his biographers wrote: 'The most striking thing about Lammy was that he packed so much strength into so little physical space. He was built for speed the lean and streamlined way, being only slightly over five feet tall and weighing just about 130 pounds.'

He was also extremely modest to the point of shyness.

Which was most uncharacteristic considering he was an American, who usually come as gaudily-packaged, loud, party animals accompanied by razzmatazz, flamboyance, colourful ostentation and suntanned sensationalism.

Well … not Wilbur Lamoreaux.

And if you believe that nice guys never win in speedway, you can forget that too. He did a lot of winning, and he was the original Mr Nice Guy, as popular wherever he went as well as with his home fans.

The first line of his entry in America's tribute to its motorcycling elite, the AMA Hall Of Fame, reads like this: 'Wilbur "Lammy" Lamoreaux was one of the best speedway racers America ever produced."

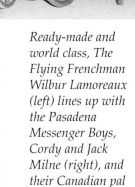

Ready-made and world class, The Flying Frenchman Wilbur Lamoreaux (left) lines up with the Pasadena Messenger Boys, Cordy and Jack Milne (right), and their Canadian pal Jimmy Gibb (second from the left).

Pre-war speedway American style: Jack Milne (No.39) and Wilbur at Los Angeles.

Wimbledon get their way in 1937. Ronnie Greene, in the smart suit and hat, secures Wilbur, in the helmet second from the right, for his Dons. From the left they are: Wally Lloyd, Nobby Key, Benny Kaufman, Fred Leavis, Eric Collins, Geoff Pymar, Nobby Clarke trainer and, on the end, Norman Evans. On the bike, manager Wal Phillips.

Below left: Set for an assault on the big prizes in British speedway, Cordy Milne, Jack Milne and Wilbur in the New Cross pits …

Below right: … And the big prizes came their way. They dominated the 1937 World Championship, Jack Milne taking the title with Wilbur, left, second and Cordy third putting the Stars And Stripes on top of the speedway world.

Wilbur, together with the Milne brothers, Jack and Cordy, burst onto the English speedway scene ready-made world class stars in the mid 1930s. There was no apprenticeship as there was to be almost half a century later with the likes of Penhall, Sigalos, Cook, King and the Morans.

Wilbur Lamoreaux and the Milnes were instant, high level international successes. Billed romantically in the 1947 edition of *Stenner's Speedway Annual* as 'Three Messenger Boys In Pasadena', none of them came from the suburb of Los Angeles. The Milnes were both born in Buffalo, New York, and Wilbur was born in Roseville, Illinois on February 26, 1907 – a mere four years after another Wilbur, Wright, and his brother Orville, had coaxed a strange contraption made of spruce, string and canvas into the air to prove that man at last had the ability to fly.

And, perhaps appropriately, Wilbur was also known as The Flying Frenchman, because of the spelling of his name, as well as being affectionately known as Lammy.

Wilbur, Jack and Cordy were all motorcycle messengers for Western Union at a time when speedway was beginning to become popular in America largely due to the success in Australia and England of the early American pioneer Lloyd 'Sprouts' Elder.

It was Elder's prowess that alerted the three messenger boys to the sport, though Wilbur had been interested in motorcycles since a teenager when he persuaded his mother to let him buy an Indian Scout.

He began riding on the half mile night tracks, starting off in San Diego, and showed great promise from the start, competing at Fresno, Long Beach, Lincoln Park and the Coliseum in Los Angeles, Saratoga and San Francisco.

His career really took off when local intrepreneur Gene Rhyne hired Wilbur to ride a Comerford JAP speedway bike originally bought from England. In 1934 and 1935 he was favourite to win the American Speedway Championship but both times he was just edged out by his friend Cordy Milne.

Wimbledon boss Ronnie Greene applied to the Speedway Control Board to bring Wilbur over for the Dons in 1935, but permission was refused. Foreign interlopers were not welcome at the time.

That year New Cross promoter Fred Mockford lost the brilliant Tom Farndon, possibly the world's best at the time, who died following a racing accident at the Old Kent Road track.

The enterprising Mockford found his star replacements in the Milne brothers and brought them over to ride in England in 1936. This time there was no objection to the Americans, but the Control Board considered that if Mockford was allowed to keep Jack and Cordy at New Cross the side would be too strong. So Cordy was allocated to the newly opened Hackney Wick.

It was the year the first official World Championship was launched and, with an indication of what was to come, Cordy Milne finished in fourth place, brother Jack was ninth.

Ronnie Greene finally secured Wilbur for Wimbledon in 1937. And Wilbur hit Plough Lane running. He turned in some superb early scores in his first season – 11 out of 12 points in the Gold Cup meeting at Wembley, 11 out of 12 in a challenge match at Bristol and 14 out of 15 in the first round of the World Championship at Wimbledon.

Though the Dons had an appalling record that year, winning only two league matches out of their 24 and finishing 16 points adrift at the foot of the First Division, Wilbur's form was outstanding. From a total of 32 league and cup matches his average was 8.53. He also scored well in the England v Overseas Test series.

The man who took Jack Milne's world title in 1938, Bluey Wilkinson, shows off his World Championship trophy in Sydney during the 1938-39 Australian season. Jack Milne is next to him, Wilbur is next and then Cordy Milne.

But the crowning glory for the three messenger boys from Pasadena was the World Final at Wembley. Jack Milne topped the qualifiers with 13 of the much criticised bonus points which riders carried with them to the Final, and went on to win the title with a 15 point maximum.

The 85,000 crowd witnessed racing of a very high standard. Wilbur, with 12 bonus points, dropped two on the night, in his third ride when he finished behind Jack Milne and Bill Kitchen. But it was enough for him to finish second, and Cordy Milne, who had qualified with 11 bonus points alongside reigning Champion Lionel Van Praag, Jack Parker and George Newton, was third.

The night, completely dominated by the Americans, put the Stars And Stripes on top of the speedway world and Jack, Wilbur and Cordy on top of the Wembley tractor celebrating the first World Final grand slam.

Next year was even better for Wilbur. His average rose to 10.61. Wimbledon did better too, winning half their league matches, beating Wembley in the National Trophy final and New Cross in the London Cup, but losing to West Ham in the ACU Cup. Wilbur again scored well in the England v USA&Canada Tests and reached the World Final.

This time West Ham's Bluey Wilkinson topped the qualifying scores with eight bonus points and, in spite of an injured shoulder, went on to win the title with 14 on the night, dropping his only point to reigning Champion Jack Milne in Heat 20.

Milne, Wilbur and Lionel Van Praag went to Wembley one bonus point behind Bluey, and that's how they finished. Milne was second and Wilbur was third, so once again there were two Americans on the podium.

It was obvious that Wilbur thrived on the British speedway scene. He was asked: 'Can you truthfully say you've learned anything from the keen competition you've met over here?'

His reply: 'I should say I have. If you want to win races here you've got to ride hard the whole time and know just as much about tactics as the best of your opponents. But they ride dead fairly and make you feel what a sporting game it all is.

'In my early days I learned a lot from someone who knew all about your English racing – Sprouts Elder. He did much to encourage me when I found it hard to make the grade.'

Wilbur just kept on getting better and better. His 1939 average went up to 10.75 which ranked him the year's top scorer with the inclusion of league and cup matches. Again he

qualified for the World Final for which Cordy Milne was favourite on eight bonus points. Once more Wilbur was one behind with Bill Kitchen and Eric Langton.

It all came to a grinding halt when war was declared just four days before the big night at Wembley. No World Championship Final and no conclusion to the league with the Dons lying second to Belle Vue having won 12 of their 18 matches. But Wilbur did have the consolation of winning the Scottish Championship.

The war years were spent on factory work and, with the Milnes and Canadian Jimmy Gibb, promoting speedway meetings along the West Coast. In 1946 Wilbur finally won the US National Championship and he raced a hugely successful 1947-48 season in Australia, leaving behind a raft of track records at the Newcastle Showground, Brisbane, the Sydney Sports Ground and the Sydney Royale. A measure of his class is in the fact that his handicap was 180 yards, when England captain and recognised number one at the time Jack Parker was on 170 yards and Jack Milne on 160 yards.

It prompted Parker, as chairman of the British Speedway Riders Association (SRA), to cable the English authorities suggesting that the Milnes and Lamoreaux should join British clubs with a view to staging the World Championship again. He was a year premature and the Americans stayed at home.

Then, early in the 1948 season, with British speedway enjoying an unprecedented boom, league champions Wembley were seriously weakened when they lost two of their heat leaders, captain Bill Kitchen with a broken arm and international George Wilks with a fractured femur.

It was Olympic year at the Empire Stadium, which meant the Lions had no track to race on. So they relocated to Wimbledon for the duration of the Games, and astute manager Alec Jackson applied to be allowed to bring over Wilbur Lamoreaux to help out. At the time, foreign riders were banned by the SRA, who were even considering restricting the Australians to two per team. But a headline in the speedway Press that proclaimed: *The SRA Says Yes To Lammy* meant the rules were relaxed because of Wembley's plight, and anyway, British speedway could not contemplate a weak Wembley.

It was hailed as a victory for common sense. But there was a proviso. In a statement the SRA said: 'This must not be regarded as a precedent for using other foreigners, and Wembley must relinquish their claim on the American rider should they … obtain the services of a recognised star rider.'

So Lammy was back and he made his debut for Wembley at his old home track at Plough Lane in an Anniversary Cup match against Belle Vue on Thursday, June 9. An account in the *Speedway Reporter* magazine said: 'Wilbut Lamoreaux, arriving from America during the morning rode in the Wembley colours and proved to be every bit as good as he was when he led the Dons' side prior to the war.

Wilbur's return after the war was as though he had never been away – he was still a world class performer and universally popular. Here he concentrates on fitting the cover on his helmet in the Belle Vue pits.

Below left: Nothing fazed the enigmatic Lammy, even the aristocracy on a visit to West Ham … deadpan Wilbur meets the Marquis of Milford Haven, who was best man at the wedding of the Queen and the Duke of Edinburgh. Eric Chitty shares the joke.

'In his first race he took the initial lap very cautiously and allowed himself to be led by (Dent) Oliver, (Wally) Lloyd and (Bob) Wells. Gradually he drove himself through the field and on the final lap swept past Oliver to win amidst great cheering.' His first two rides – he won them both – were described as 'masterful examples of high class track tactics.'

In his third, an eagerly awaited meeting with visiting captain Jack Parker, he threw a chain at the start. There was another win, and a third behind Parker and Split Waterman in the final heat for 10 points. Though Wembley lost 51 – 45, Wilbur had made a highly satisfactory, and popular, return. Wembley fans dedicated a song to him. To the tune of the Al Jolson hit *Mammy* they sang: I'd go a million miles for one of your rides, my La-a-a-ammy.'

In the substitute World Championship, the Speedway Riders Championship, the opening qualifying round was at Wimbledon, and Wilbur beat the virtually invincible Vic Duggan to take the £60 winner's cheque with a 15-point maximum. Duggan, on 57 out of 60 points, led the qualifiers for the Final, back at Wembley with the Empire Stadium once again available following the Olympics. Norman Parker was next on 52 and Wilbur third highest qualifier with 49.

Though the Lions surrendered their league title to New Cross, Wilbur had helped them to win the National Trophy and the London Cup. But the Championship Final night was a disaster. His chances were virtually ended as early as his first ride in a Heat 3 crash with Ron Johnson. Both of them were thrown heavily into the fence and Wilbur's machine was wrecked. Riding a borrowed spare he ended the night with three seconds and two lasts for six points and ninth place overall. Johnson went on to finish second to champion Duggan with Alec Statham third.

Wilbur was universally popular, though a reader's letter in the speedway Press, under the headline *The Lamoreaux Question*, revealed a growing resentment against a perceived Wembley bias. Mr F.A. Coombs of Willesden wrote: 'Wilbur Lamoreaux should be

Below right: There was one more season in Britain for Wilbur, in 1949 to strengthen Birmingham, newly promoted to the First Division. From the left: Doug McLachlan, Fred Perkins, Dennis Hitchings, Wilbur, Bill Wilkins, Arthur Payne, Geoff Bennett, Graham Warren, Dick Tolley, Buck Whitby and Brian Wilson. Captain Stan Dell is on the machine.

The pocket dynamo, perfectly balanced on the inside of the more fiery Cyril Roger at New Cross, displaying all the elegance of his classy style.

dropped now that Bill Kitchen has returned to the Lions. In the first place they should never have had the benefit of his services. Wembley have had preferential treatment on many occasions. I wonder what football supporters would say if the Players Union insisted that Arsenal should be top dogs and let them have all the best players?'

The editorial response was that not only should Wembley be allowed to keep Wilbur, but all the Americans should be invited over and shared out among the teams. 'The richest football clubs get the best players', pointed out the Editor.

So no change there then.

But Wembley did not keep Wilbur. In 1949 he went to Birmingham, newly promoted to the First Division thanks largely to the sensationally brilliant Graham Warren. The

Three wise men … Wembley's Alec Jackson, Birmingham boss Les Marshall (centre) and Wilbur – Mr Cool – contemplate the happenings out on the track.

Brummies were always going to struggle, but Wilbur, at 40, was as good as ever, lowering Jack Parker's record at Belle Vue early in the season and, with Warren and to a lesser extent Arthur Payne, scoring most of the points for the Perry Bar side.

Wilbur's racing career was virtually injury free, apart from some ankle damage. One of these came in July in a crash against visiting Harringay. Wilbur appeared to be bundled off by Danny Dunton and slid almost the length of the back straight under his machine, coming to rest over the concrete curb.

The crowd blamed Dunton for the accident and forever afterwards he was known at Perry Barr as Dirty Danny Dunton.

It didn't stop Wilbur for long. With the World Championship reinstated, he became an instant favourite for the title by winning his first qualifying round at Wembley In August with a 15 point maximum after an epic ride to beat nearest rival Wembley's Bill Gilbert. But the Final, in front of 93,000, proved to be another unhappy night.

In his first ride he was leading eventual runner-up Jack Parker when Dent Oliver went down and took Parker with him. In the re-run – as so often happens – Parker got the drop and Wilbur was second. Parker's brother Norman took another point from him in his second ride but he won his third. His fourth, in Heat 12, his second on the run, was a disaster against eventual 'lucky' Champion Tommy Price of Wembley, Ron Clarke of Bradford and Aub Lawson of West Ham.

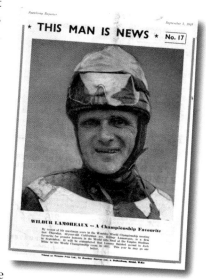

Tom Stenner's report in his 1950 annual read: 'Tommy's luck came in his third ride when, after twice being passed by Lamoreaux, he was running a challenging third behind Ron Clarke. The race seemed a Lamoreaux certainty, but an oiled up plug caused an engine cut-out on the corner entering lap four. Lamoreaux drifted out and Clarke, trying to guess which way the American would go, went wider still. In nipped Price, and that was that.'

Wilbur's scoring over the two post-war years were amazingly consistent. His league average was 9.71 for Wembley and 9.891 for Birmingham. As some sort of consolation for his World Championship disappointment, in October Wilbur went on to win the Tom Farndon Memorial Trophy at New Cross in a line-up that included the World Final top three, Price, Parker and Parker's Belle Vue team mate Louis Lawson. So perhaps there was some sort of poetic justice in his victory.

This is how Speedway Reporter *magazine put forward its choice of Wilbur as the favourite for the 1949 World Championship title … it was not the only section of the speedway Press to fancy Lammy's chances.*

But it was his final farewell. In October too, the pound was devalued which, Wilbur said, halved his earnings potential in England. *Speedway Reporter* commented: 'The American has a genuine moan … here he could buy a pound of beef for half a crown (12.5pence). A similar piece of beef in America would cost a dollar – five shillings (25pence) before devaluation.'

Wilbur said: 'The only possible way I could earn a living from my track earnings would be to settle down permanently in England. And though I regard this country as my second home, there's no place like the real thing, so at the end of the season it will be California here I come … '

He went back, never to return. There was a motorcycle business and a property portfolio. A heavy smoker, Wilbur died in May 1963. He was fifty-six.

We are indebted to John Warner and Peter Jackson's Speedway Archives for Wilbur's scoring statistics.

Wilbur's post-war high status was recognised by him being nominated to challenge for Jack Parker's British Match Race Championship. He didn't take the Golden Helmet from Jack, but he did lower the maestro's Belle Vue track record, and here he has the better of Jack in a league encounter.

Tommy Price
THE TOUGH OF THE TRACK

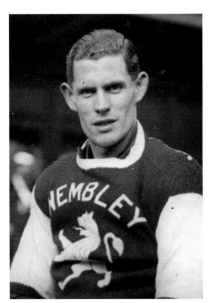

A young Tommy in his Wembley Lions sweater.

NO LESS A PERSON than the Old Warhorse himself, Johnnie H Hoskins, took the young and eager Tommy Price aside and told him to forget about trying to make speedway his profession because he would never make the grade.

Johnnie should have known better.

Tommy Price eventually became one of the most successful stars of the fabulous Wembley Lions super-team of the late pre-war and early post-war years, and Hoskins was proved spectacularly wrong at Wembley Stadium on the incident and drama-packed night of Thursday, 22 September 1949 when Tommy did make the grade to become World Champion with an immaculate 15 point maximum.

Everything about Tommy was always immaculate. From his highly burnished leathers to the way he looked after his mechanical equipment.

In a special edition of *Vintage Speedway Magazine* to mark speedway's 70th birthday at the beginning of 1998 I wrote an appreciation of Tommy's career and headlined it *The Tough Of The Track*. Because that's what Tommy was … the tough guy of the track. He was not only physically tough, but mentally tough as well.

Tommy Price was the first World Champion I interviewed, and I hadn't been in his company very long before it became obvious he had supreme confidence in his own ability. He was highly motivated and, not only that, he was highly opinionated as well.

They were attributes I came to recognise within every other holder of the title World Speedway Champion I have had the good fortune and privilege to meet and interview over the decades.

The word most used by speedway people recalling the life and brilliant times of Thomas Hubert Price is: hard. He was a hard man, they said. Other words they used were: determined and dedicated. The dedication was directed particularly to mechanical excellence, and most certainly to winning.

When I put his 'hard man' reputation to him he said: 'Well, you had to be hard, didn't you? If you wanted to succeed at being a speedway rider you had to be hard.'

Could it have been the harsh comment by Hoskins which proved to be the spark that ignited in Tommy Price a furnace of fierce pride and propelled him to the very pinnacle of speedway stardom.

One of his caustic and apparently cynical comments was: 'The surest way to be unpopular is to win the World Championship.'

Cynical? Maybe, but it was something that Tommy Price learned the hard way – sorry to use *that* word again. But it was the nature of the man. There is the story, sworn to be absolutely true by some, and vehemently denied by others, that at one time Tommy was so unpopular with his own Wembley team mates that he was banned from their dressing room. He had to arrive at a meeting in leathers or use the opposing team's dressing room.

He had – shall we say – a certain on-track reputation. Away from the track he could not have been a more pleasant human being. Whatever the public and professional view of him was, it cannot be denied that he is one of the most admired competitors the sport has ever known. He did, after all, earn his place in the pantheon of speedway history, immortalised by being the first Englishman to become World Speedway Champion.

Veteran Jim Gregory, one of the legion of young hopefuls watching starry-eyed as Tommy burst into world class prominence in that unforgettably magical boom time for the sport during those first few post-war years, bestows upon him what would probably be regarded as the ultimate accolade. Jim says: 'He wasn't unsporting or anything, but if he went for a spot he got it. I was a novice at the time and he was a star – one of the all-time greats. He was a god to us – one of the gods.'

It was not always so. But if Tommy Price exhibited uncompromising qualities, it was born of necessity. Charlie May, one of his team mates in that magnificent Wembley championship-winning side of 1946, said: 'He had to win. I had ridden beside him, but you were in the way. With Tommy you had to move over and let him through.'

Tommy saw it as 'my ferocious determination'.

Freddie Williams, also a wide-eyed Wembley newcomer at the time, and eventually a double World Champion, said: 'He wasn't very nice to know on the track. Off it he was wonderful – he was a sort of Jekyll and Hyde character. Tommy and Bill Kitchen, our captain, used to come to the training sessions at Rye House to help youngsters like me. We were only kids, but he and Bill were terrific to us when we were really a bit of a nuisance. We were, after all, trying to take their places in the team. I have nothing but praise for him – but I can respect the fact that on the track all he was interested in was winning.'

Winning was what was always required at Wembley. Insisted upon by the man who ran the place, Sir Arthur Elvin. To him an unsuccessful Wembley team was not an option.

Fred said: 'I couldn't say Tommy was a team man, until later on in his career. There was

The Champ: That's the trophy for winning the World Championship substitute, the 1946 British Riders Championship. It made him a real star and he was hailed as 'Giant Killing Lion Of The Season' … but the best was yet to come.

a saying about Tommy and his team partner: "You can have any gate position you like as long as he has No. 1."

'Tommy was ruthless and hard (*there's that word again*). He wouldn't give an inch to anyone, and it never upset me except when he knocked my brother Eric off a few times. I wouldn't ride with Eric because it always seemed to result in a crash. So he usually ended up with Tommy – and Tommy used to knock him off.'

The young Reg Fearman was just making his way with West Ham at the time. He insists that the story of Tommy's exclusion from the team dressing room is true, and said: 'I remember him for his racing ability of course, and his success. I beat him for the odd point at Wembley once. I was looking over my shoulder coming out of every corner and I could see his eyes through his goggles. It was not like it is today, we just wore a handkerchief round the mouth and you could see a man's eyes. Tommy's eyes were out. He was determined to get me. And when I did cross the line in front of him I breathed a great sigh of relief.

'When we got back to the pits he came over to me and said: "A very good ride, son." And from then on we were friends. He was a great rider and a great man of his time.'

The Price apprenticeship to greatness was down a long and winding road. Born in Cambridge in 1911, he blamed his father for making him 'motorcycle mad'. He was given a miniature bike at the age of eight and he inherited his mechanical skill from his father. 'I had a passion for all things mechanical,' Tommy admitted, and it carried him to worldwide fame.

He began his working life with the Associated Equipment Company, which built London buses. He said later that it was what he learned there that refined his mechanical knowledge and skill.

His racing apprenticeship started on the grass track. At his first meeting at St Ives, in Cambridgeshire, there was an incident that was enough to scare off anyone with ambitions to motorcycling fame – a rider was killed in the first race. As if that wasn't enough to make Tommy reconsider his choice of career, on the way home he was in an accident with a bunch of female cyclists and broke his left leg. Fortunately none of the girls was hurt.

Undeterred, as soon as he was fit again, he began competing in meetings at the grass-speedway at Barnet in north London, where one day in 1934 top Australian Test star Frank Arthur happened to be among the spectators.

Arthur was with Harringay then and he was impressed enough with Tommy and George Wilks, who was also to become an international with England and Wembley, to arrange for them to have a trial in a junior event.

Tommy led the race for three laps, then, he said: 'I overslid and while I was picking myself up George Wilks sailed past to win. As a result of that George was signed by Harringay, I was politely thanked for going along, and I returned to grass tracking.

But, he said: 'You can learn so much from grass tracking. I regard it as the most instructive step to the cinders.'

As well as Barnet, he was also riding at Luton, then a nursery track for Wembley's Second Division junior team, and became friends with George Hannaford, an Australian who also rode in the Isle of Man TT races. In 1936 George had a crash during the TTs, fracturing his skull. He stayed at the Price home to recover and, as he was not fit enough to turn out for the young Lions, asked Wembley manager Alec Jackson if Tommy could take his place.

Jackson agreed, and this time there as no mistake, no over-eager fall, and Tommy top scored. He impressed Jackson so much that he put Tommy in the novices' race at the Empire Stadium which he won for the next six weeks in a row.

It was the launch of his career at Wembley that would endure until Elvin's death when his successors shut down league speedway after the 1956 season. But first Tommy was loaned out to Cardiff. It would not be the last time he would be banished from the glamour of the metropolis.

A study in concentration: Tommy satisfying himself that nothing is left to chance. Everything about his equipment had to be perfect.

He was back in the big time in 1937 and a team that included big names: Lionel Van Praag, the reigning World Champion and internationals Ginger Lees, Wally Kilmister and Frank Charles who took an interest in the emerging Tommy. One of his pieces of advice was that Tommy should convert his leg-trailing style to the more efficient foot-forward style favoured by Charles. The northerner became something of a hero to Tommy.

Wembley finished runners-up to West Ham in the league that year, and though the side seemed to be condemned to being also-rans – losing to New Cross in the National Trophy semi-final and Belle Vue in the AC-U Cup final – manager Jackson appeared happy with the way things were going, commenting: 'We have been regarded as fortunate in that Cliff Parkinson, Wally Lloyd and Tommy Price are showing such brilliant form. Folk appear to have overlooked the fact that Wembley has persevered with these three riders. Tommy Price, our latest discovery, has the Wembley interests at heart. He is a most conscientious lad, and he has listened to advice. Price is on the upgrade.'

He certainly was. The following season he qualified for the first of his four World Finals. He went to the Final with just four of the infamous bonus points and finished with only four extra from his rides, but he was twelfth among the top 16 in the world and they included Bluey Wilkinson, who won, Jack and Cordy Milne, Wilbur Lamoreaux, team mate Van Praag, Eric Langton, Jack Parker, Arthur Atkinson and Bill Kitchen.

In the ominous year of 1939 there was no World Final qualification but there were two appearances for England against the Australians. In the first Test at New Cross and what

turned out to be the fifth and final Test at Wembley when he really made his international mark with three wins. A sixth Test had been planned for the series, which was to have been on 19 September at West Ham but, as with the World Championship Final, it was never held. Everything stopped for a war.

Tommy was a keen short-wave radio enthusiast, and during the war was attached to the United States Parachute corps, the 101st Airborne Division, lecturing on radio engineering and showing combat and instructional films to the troops while still racing.

He was able to carry on racing because, of course, not everything did stop for the war. Belle Vue kept the speedway wheels turning at weekends. As with several other aspiring younger riders such as Ron Clarke, Oliver Hart, Alec Statham and Eric Chitty, riding against the top stars week after week during the war years really put the final polish on Tommy Price.

For the gallant band who kept things going throughout the duration of hostilities, the Hyde Road meetings were often chaotic – and not only for Belle Vue manager Alice Hart who had to organise the whole thing.

Riders travelling to Manchester by train had to deal with antagonistic railway staff who would often take to unloading bikes and dumping them back on the platform just as the train was pulling out of the station.

The boys eventually took to riding with their precious machines in the guard's van. And they would sit there waiting for one of them to be first to open his sandwich bag. They always tried to wait for Tommy because he usually had the best selection.

It was in 1945 that Tommy began to win things. There was the Belle Vue Speedway Derby Best Pairs with Jack Parker, he was runner-up with Eric Chitty in the British Individual Championship and the outright winner of the Belle Vue Grand Prix.

Normal speedway racing was resumed in 1946. But it wasn't really normal. An entertainment starved pubic poured into meetings in vast turnstile-busting numbers.

Wembley prepared for an opening night crowd of 80,000. In the event it was 50,000 who saw the Lions overwhelm Belle Vue 50 – 32 in a National League match. Tommy Price top scored with 11 points, dropping his only point to maximum man Jack Parker.

A downpour of rain the following week kept the crowd down to 43,000 against visiting Wimbledon. Tommy again scored 11 in a 48 – 35 victory. But a record 65,000 turned up for the next match, a 54 – 34 win over New Cross, in which Tommy rode to a four-ride, 12 point maximum, as did Bill Kitchen and George Wilks.

Speedway News reported: 'This win gave Wembley a clear two point lead at the head of the league table and they will take a lot of displacing.' It was an accurate prediction: Wembley finished as champions a handsome 10 points clear above Belle Vue.

And before an 85,000 crowd Tommy Price finished as the individual champion. He won the World Championship substitute, the British Riders Championship and was hailed as 'Giant Killing Lion Of The Season'.

He won it, of course, on his home track, Wembley, something from which he would ever be able to escape. His detractors called him lucky … well, maybe. Favourite Parker, challenging Price when they met in Heat 6, was brought down when the leather strap on his steel shoe broke.

Tommy was magnanimous enough to confess after the meeting: 'I had all the luck going. I owe a great deal to Cyril Spinks for super-tuning my motor and to Jack Parker for the advice he gave me when I was building a frame a couple of months back.'

What he didn't say was that he had been suffering from concussion for almost two weeks before the Final after crashing in his last qualifying round at Belle Vue.

Whatever: his win elevated him to second place behind Parker in the national rankings and to third place in the World Rankings behind Vic Duggan and Parker. His transfer value was put at a contemporary £25,000 which, in today's values, is equivalent to a staggering £550,000-plus.

With the re-emergence of speedway as a major popular entertainment the Wembley juggernaught bulldozed on, winning seven of the next eight league championships. The season they failed to do so was 1948 when they had to ride most of their 'home' meetings at Wimbledon because the Olympic Games took over the Empire Stadium.

Below left: The Price of fame … Tommy is the main attraction at Olympia helping to promote speedway and the Sunday Despatch, *the paper that backed the British Champion-ship he won in 1946 and went on to sponsor the World Championship when it was revived three years later.*

Above right: The Wembley Lions super-team line-up of 1947 on parade before racing, with the packed Empire Stadium terraces behind. From the left Bronco Wilson, Tommy, Bill Gilbert, George Wilks, Bill Kitchen, Split Waterman and Charlie May.

Tommy was the rider Wimbledon fans loved to hate and he harboured a permanent dislike for promoter Ronnie Greene who refused to compensate him for the damage Dons supporters did to his new car when they attacked it with iron bars. He took permanent revenge by attaching a picture of Greene to the underside of his toilet seat.

Tommy took over as captain when Bill Kitchen was injured and there was a measure of compensation for Wembley when, back in their proper home, they beat 1948 champions New Cross in both the London Cup and National Trophy finals.

As befitted Tommy's top flight status he was nominated to challenge Jack Parker for the Golden Helmet three times between 1946 and 1950 but each time he lost to the Match Race maestro.

Perhaps it was poetic justice that he prevented Parker from the supreme title not once but twice. First, in their dramatic meeting in the British Riders Championship in 1946, and finally in the 1949 World Final, again at Wembley.

Parker was getting older, he was 44 – the same age as American Greg Hancock when he won his third world title in 2014 – and winning the World Championship would have crowned a magnificent career. Jack was barely able to conceal that it was a matter of bitter regret that the official title had always eluded him.

And so, to that fateful Thursday night in September 1949. There were two more World Finals to come, but the reality was it was his very last chance.

Fred Williams put it down to Jack's well-known disposition to be what he called 'slap-happy about his equipment'. Fred said: 'We would all arrive for a World Final with immaculate bikes. We'd look at Parker's and it would be filthy and there would be rollers missing from his chains. His machines would be a shambles. I don't know how he rode them.'

Parker had carefully perpetrated the myth that he was able to pick up any old bike lying around the pits and go out and beat the world on it. His racing philosophy could not have been further from Tommy Price's.

But the road to the Final for Tommy started out a long way from Wembley. Just like at the start of his career when he was sent to the provinces, his early season form was such that manager Jackson didn't seed him into the First Division Championship Round. Tommy had to ride in the Third Round at Second Division Newcastle.

Maybe it was a wake-up call, but he made it through and then led the First Division qualifiers with Birmingham's Graham Warren on 38 points.

He was coming into form at the right time. In the week of the Final there had been three maximums within twenty-four hours and a 16 league race winning run in four days. It was not too surprising that sections of the speedway Press were tipping him for the title. His preparation, as usual, was meticulous. He

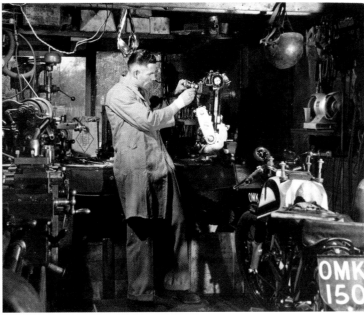

More concentration … and dedication … far from the speedway track: Tommy – 'a most conscientious lad' – in his temple to mechanical excellence where all the meticulous preparation was done.

was careful about his diet and, he said: 'I locked myself in my workshop for three days completely rebuilding two machines.'

Yet the omens for the big night were not exactly favourable. For a start he was drawn at No.13, and thirteen days before he had lost to Parker in their Golden Helmet decider at Harringay following a third bout of concussion, the latest after a crash the previous night at Wembley.

As In the run-up to his championship win in 1946, he spent the morning practising starts in the Wembley car park, and had annoyed people living close to the stadium.

When he arrived in the pits he caused some amusement among his rivals because he was carrying four spare wheels with a brand new tyre on each one. He said: 'I knew my equipment was in perfect condition and I wanted to have a new tyre for each of my rides.' The practice is common today, but was unconventional then.

He was supremely confident, a confidence boosted no doubt because the majority of the 93,000 crowd was made up – naturally – of his home track supporters. And they were about to witness one of the most incident-packed and controversial Finals in the short history of the World Championship.

Tommy's riding number – an ominous 13 – called for two consecutive rides early in the meeting, in heats 4 and 5, and in Heat 5 was the high-scoring Warren. But he won them both.

The magic moment on 22 September 1949 when Tommy Price earned himself speedway immortality by becoming the first Englishman to put his name on the World Championship trophy. Mrs Violet Attlee, wife of the then Prime Minister, makes the presentation …

Meanwhile, Parker had run into trouble as early as his opening ride in Heat 2. Danger man American Wilbur Lamoreaux, was leading comfortably when Parker and his Belle Vue team mate Dent Oliver crashed and the race had to be re-run with the exclusion of Oliver.

Parker sustained an ankle injury in the collision, but though he went on to defeat Lamoreaux in the re-run it was, reported Basil Storey in *Speedway Gazette*, 'the beginning of the Parker misadventures … and curtains for Lamoreaux'. Parker's injury was bad enough for him to pull out of the meeting at Harringay the following night after two rides.

Tommy's third ride in Heat 12 was crucial. He was overtaken by Lamoreaux and Tommy even dropped back to third as Ron Clarke also got the better of him. Then Lamoreaux stopped on the back straight of the last lap with an oiled up sparking plug. Clarke, confused by the wavering Lamoreaux, went out wide which allowed Tommy through to win.

Parker's misadventures persisted in the following heat. He was being challenged by Warren when Graham fell and Jack's brother Norman, who was following, put down his bike to avoid a serious accident.

… And the Speedway World *newspaper makes the announcement.*

Jack had to win the race all over again and then face Tommy in the very next race. Both faced the tapes unbeaten and the massive crowd was obviously acutely aware that Heat 14 was going to decide the title.

Tommy made the best start and got away ahead of his Wembley team mate Bill Gilbert followed by Parker. It was two laps before Jack was able to get past Gilbert and by then it was too late. Parker fans accused Gilbert of deliberately holding him back to help Tommy, but others suggested that eleven consecutive laps had proved too much for Parker.

All Tommy had to do was win his last ride in Heat 19 to become World Champion.

It was a unique night for British speedway, the top four places were taken by English riders; Tommy Price, Jack Parker, Louis Lawson, who had claimed third place almost unnoticed as the drama unfolded, and Jack's brother Norman.

Tommy excused himself from the post Final dinner, even declining to be tempted by the offer of Arthur Elvin's chauffeur driven limousine, to go home. He had promised to call a blind fellow radio ham to tell him all about how he had become World Champion.

Pop star status: Tommy gets the treatment from enthusiastic autograph-hunting fans who crowd the pit rails at Wembley to get close to their idol.

And this is what he treated them to … a typically polished virtuoso solo performance.

Proud father: Tommy with wife Margaret and newly born daughter Melanie.

Tommy negotiates a water feature spectacularly on the first bend at Harringay – he was in the lead, as usual, from Split Waterman, outside, partner Eric Williams and Ron How.

Speedway wasn't Tommy Price's only motorcycling talent, he was an accomplished road racer as well.

The following night he was also at Harringay, as newly crowned World Champion, but declined to raise his previously agreed £50 appearance fee because of his new status.

Tommy Price's racing career ended at the age of forty-five with the closing of Wembley at the end of 1956, but also, he said, because the crowds had ceased to boo him.

Almost a decade later as British speedway entered what is now known as the modern era, he was back … as manager of the re-opened West Ham. The Price magic was undimmed, and in 1965 he guided the Hammers to a League, Knock Out Cup and London Cup treble.

He finally retired to Western Australia, where he died aged 86 in January 1998. There was a suggestion that Tommy's wife Margaret would bring his ashes back to England. But when I asked her, she said: 'John, he is still in Australia – a country he really loved.'

Even after his riding days were done, Tommy Price was not finished with speedway, he was back to guide West Ham to a triple triumph, championship of the new amalgamated British League, the Knock Out Cup and the London Cup in 1965. The team on a lap of honour are, from the left: Norman Hunter, Tony Clarke, Sverre Harrfeldt, Malcolm Simmons and Ken McKinlay. In front Brian Leonard and Reg Trott. Tommy is holding the league championship trophy.

Tommy Price's Career Record

World Champion 1949

British Champion 1946

World Finals 1938 12th, 1949 1st, 1950 5th, 1954 11th

Internationals 23, points 181

National League Championships 1946, Division 1: 1947, 1949, 1950, 1951, 1952, 1953
National Trophy 1948, 1954

Ranked one of Wembley's best and most consistent riders scoring almost 3,000 points in the eleven post-war years.

Sir Arthur to the Rescue

Wembley's chief Sir Arthur Elvin MBE had, from speedway's very earliest days, supported the sport.

He was often described as the best friend speedway ever had.

Elvin, a First World War Royal Flying Corps veteran, never hesitated to put his money where his mouth was – apart, apparently, from rewarding his World Championship winning contracted riders with anything over and above what was officially permitted *(See Page 159)*.

His value to the sport was incalculable. In the days when the nation's morning newspapers gave speedway space on their sports pages, one leading journalist put it down to the fact that Fleet Street's editors 'saw that Elvin was in it, so it must be OK'.

And so, when he agreed to his Empire Stadium being used for the 1948 London Olympics, rather than see his Lions with no track to race on he leased Wimbledon.

Speedway Reporter magazine editor Len Steed revealed: 'Sir Arthur Elvin is one of the backbones of the sport in this country, and rather than close down the speedway until Wembley reopens Sir Arthur runs consistently every week at a loss.

Speedway News *magazine announces the honour in its issue dated 20 June 1946.*

'It would be easy for him to refuse to lose money any more, but speedway cannot afford to have the Lions close down their shop even temporarily.'

Elvin was awarded a knighthood in the Royal Honours List of June 1946. He died aged only 57 in February 1957 on a cruise ship off Madeira and was buried at sea. Almost before the waves had closed over his body the people he had ruled over as chairman and managing director of Wembley Stadium handed a statement to the speedway authorities to say that they were closing Wembley to league racing.

George Newton
BOY GEORGE RIDES AGAIN

FORGIVE ME for permitting myself a mild indulgence. I don't normally do requests, but I just couldn't resist an appeal to recall the meteoric and spectacular speedway career of George Newton.

The very mention of the name of Wee Georgie had me taking a nostalgic trip down the years to the vicinity of the Old Kent Road in south-east London where, along with those other cinders artists from the sport's glorious past, Tom Farndon, Jack Milne, Ron Johnson, Bill Longley and Stan Greatrex, used to practise their craft.

The request came in a letter from A. Pearson of New Milton in Hampshire. I was left to contemplate whether A. Pearson was Mr, Ms or Mrs. It had me in mind of the days when A. Pearson said he/she was being thrilled by what he/she described as 'the great sport in its halcyon days', when letters were usually signed more formally than they are in the IT Facebook/Twitter times like these.

The spirits of legend, Fred Mockford's boys at Crystal Palace in the sport's halcyon days … the late Thirties. George, at the very start of his career, is on the far right. Fred's boys are, from the left: Triss Sharp, Joe Francis, Nobby Key, Ron Johnson, Tom Farndon and Harry Shepherd. Fred is in the hat.

Times 'like these' – in case you hadn't noticed – are also the days of da-glo Kevlar racing suits, guests, laydown engines, small back wheels, black and white helmet covers, double-points tacticals and Jokers. It did strike me that his/her request for something on such a great New Cross favourite as the boy George meant he/she had to be a man/woman after my own heart.

Well, you only have to look at the other stars of the era mentioned in A. Pearson's missive – Jack Parker, Norman Parker, Bill Kitchen, Eric Langton – to contemplate that he/she may have stirred the spirits of legend into riding again a few ghostly laps around the grassy children's playground that was once New Cross speedway stadium.

The echoes of the great crowds that once streamed along Ilderton Road to the place that inspired the film, *Once A Jolly Swagman*, starring Dirk Bogarde, no less, and Bill 'Compo' Owen too, may well have grown silent, but there are some who say they can still hear the spectral roar of the speedway motors that for so long thrilled the multitude of Rangers fans every Wednesday night.

And long before the slogan was hijacked/pirated by certain American and certain Poole promoters, it really was *The Only Reason For Wednesday Nights*.

One of those speedway motors had George Newton astride it. Well, when I say astride, more often than not he was hanging off it, furiously leg-trailing his way round the fence of The Old Frying Pan, as the tiny 262yd track was known, spraying with cinders his loyal devotees in their black and orange favours.

Wee Georgie was nothing if not a sensational crowd pleaser. He was a natural successor to the great Tom Farndon, who had met a tragic death after crashing with team mate Ron Johnson on the very eve of the Star Championship Final at Wembley in 1935. Farndon was the reigning British Champion, the holder of no end of track records throughout the country and probably the best speedway rider in the world at the time.

But it was three years earlier, when New Cross bosses Fred Mockford and Cecil Smith were running Crystal Palace, that George, then a lad little more than seventeen years old, walked in on Messrs Mockford and Smith and asked for a trial.

Now the firm of Mockford & Smith were never ones to pass up a likely lad. They had pioneered the sport at the Palace since 1928, even giving rides to a woman – Fay Taylour – in the very early days.

George got his trial, and the story is that within days he was in the Crystal Palace team. Even his debut was a bit of a sensation. In his second ride he equalled Vic Huxley's two-year-old track record – and Australian Huxley was a sort of Ivan Mauger / Tony Rickardsson of the day – or, if you are really modern, a Tai Woffinden / Greg Hancock.

In George's first international, the opening Test at Wembley against Australia in 1936, he scored a cool 16 points – two off a maximum against the world's best – helping England to a 65 – 43 win. He was in the first race of the first World Final in 1936, unfortunately he was last behind Frank Charles, Dick Case and Wal Phillips and overall finishing an unlucky thirteenth. Two more pre-war World Finals followed.

Mockford and Smith moved the Crystal Palace side to New Cross in 1934 and George helped the Rangers to their first League title in 1938. By 1939 he held four New Cross track records, the four laps with Arthur Atkinson, the one lap flying start with 1937 World Champion Jack Milne and team mate Stan Greatrex, and the two and four laps flying start on his own.

Portrait of a lad of seventeen with ambition.

Below: *Making his mark already … George is selected to join a representative side of southerners in a North v South trial to choose an England team for a Test series against Australia. From the left: Colin Watson, George, Gus Kuhn, Harold 'Tiger' Stevenson, Tommy Croombs, Nobby Key, Tom Farndon and Jack Parker.*

A happy band of Rangers, the 1936 New Cross side with Norman 'Pansy' Evans on the far left, then Mike Erskine, George, Ron Johnson, Stan Greatrex, Fred Mockford, Jack Milne and Nobby Key.

Two great, but differing, talents: George shakes hands with one of the masters, Eric Langton.

But his career was held back by a 'mystery illness' – tuberculosis, as A. Pearson so rightly said. It was an illness talked about in hushed tones for some reason in those days, and the nature of George's problem was never fully revealed in the speedway prints of the time, but it was said that he had to have one lung removed

After the war George made a brave comeback with his old club New Cross in 1948, riding under the handicap of having only one lung and scoring only 35 points. After more hospital treatment he took his harum-scarum, fence-scraping style to Second Division Fleetwood in 1949 where his 327 league points put him in the top bracket with the likes of Ken LeBreton of Ashfield, Alan Hunt of Cradley Heath and Bob Oakley of Southampton. He outscored even the great Jack Young of Edinburgh that year.

On to Walthamstow in 1950, never compromising his full-bore leg-trailing displays as a concession to the new shale track surfaces. He joined Liverpool alongside a raw young novice named Peter Craven in 1951 and 1952, but age was catching up with him and the points were harder and harder to come by.

Here is how he described his attempt to resume his track career in 1949: 'I never thought after my first comeback that I would ever get astride a bike again. After my New Cross re-debut had reached an inglorious end, everyone, myself included, thought that it was "curtains" for me as far as the cinders game was concerned.

Ready for action at the Old Frying Pan: George on track at New Cross preparing to please the crowds filling the terracing behind him.

'When I did get out of hospital I looked around for something to do. My whole life had been connected with speedway, I didn't want to change its course. So I decided to take a stab at it again.

'I had a trial ride. Any ill effects and that would have been finish. I felt stiff. After my layoff it would have been amazing to have felt otherwise. Apart from that, nothing. So I decided on comeback number two. When I announced it there was something of a commotion among my friends, but after all I was the one who was going to have to do the riding, so they let me get on with it.

'Advice showered in from all quarters. Some felt it was the strain of riding First Division with New Cross that had caused my last bit of trouble. It was thought that I'd be better off in the Second Division where, I was told, the pace wasn't quite so fast. Let me say that is the biggest fallacy I've ever heard. You try keeping men like Bruce Semmens, Paddy Mills, Billy Hole or Jack Young behind you for four laps. They go plenty fast. And so do you if you want to keep earning.

'At first, dropping down a grade didn't appeal to me. I didn't want to be considered a "has been", and a million and one other notions flitted through my brain – all against such a move. But I went. And I'm glad.

'My first meeting was at Bristol. We got 22 points between us. I got three. I came away thinking if this is normal Second Division racing, the sooner I get back to the Old Kent Road the better. My second meeting, at Newcastle, left me with a maximum. I managed the same thing against the same lads two days later in my first meeting at Fleetwood. That brought my confidence back, and with my average at around the eight point mark by the end of May, and steadily rising, I consider my comeback a success. If it hadn't been I don't think I'd have stuck the game. I'd hate to be riding because folks were being sympathetic.

'I find, in my tours round the various tracks, that there are still people who regard leg-trailing as either just showy, or plain dangerous. I'm not going to say that foot-forward is not the steadier of the two styles, I do however think trailing is just as fast and as safe. That can be proven by the fact that I broke the track record at Walthamstow, a small circuit which isn't exactly a trailer's cup of tea. From what I remember about First Division racing, Oliver hart isn't exactly standing still either.

'Granted a trailer looks as though he is going to fall at any moment, but skilful use of balance enables him to lay his machine down to the correct angle – and recover while keeping a reasonable full throttle. By this means he can keep driving all the way round a bend. And a good trailer can white line with the best of them – just watch Olly Hart in particular.

The spectacle that drew in fabulous crowds in what used to be called The Good Old Days – two classic artists of the leg-trailing style, George, on the inside, goes wheel to wheel with Oliver Hart.

George had to take a break from racing because of his illness, but was able to present the Tom Farndon Memorial Trophy to Jeff Lloyd in 1947.

'Maybe it's the relative scarcity of good trailers that keeps them popular with the public. Ask any fan which they prefer watching. I've no doubt who will win. The trailers every time.'

Wee Georgie has been gone now for some years. But, thanks to A. Pearson, whether Mr, Ms or Mrs, for requesting a trip back to a time when those definitely were the days.

And a stray thought occurred to me: Pearson. Now I thought the name was somewhat familiar. I don't suppose … no, it couldn't be … he/she is related to that chap off the television speedway channel by any chance?

Speedway is showbiz … and just after the war the sport attracted the biggest stars, on this occasion in 1949 the ukelele king and long-time speedway fan George Formby (in the shades) and his wife Beryl visited Fleetwood. George is sitting on the far right. Other speedway notables in the group include Dennis Parker, Frank Malouf, Norman Hargreaves, Ernie Appleby, Danny Lee, Frank Varey, Clem Mitchell, Jack Young, Cyril Cooper and Dick Campbell.

George, who moved to Liverpool in 1951, refused to compromise his full-bore trailing style, even when cinder tracks gave way to shale, and here he disputes the lead with like-minded trailer the veteran Wilf Jay, then with Fleetwood.

Before switching to Liverpool, George spent a season with Walthamstow Wolves and he lined-up with , from the left: Jimmy Grant, Reg Reeves, Archie Windmill, Jim Boyd, Benny King, George, John Deeley manager, Harry Edwards, and Charlie May.

Bob Andrews

SPEEDWAY'S WALKING DISASTER ZONE

When Bob Andrews set out to be a star of the speedways, he appeared to be somewhat lacking in what might be considered the basic essentials. He turned up for a trial at Wimbledon with no bike, no proper leathers and no steel shoe. He did have a helmet.

A walking disaster zone that was Bob. For one thing, it should have occurred to him that he had chosen the wrong career path, because the raw power of a 500cc speedway machine frightened him. There were other things too. He claims to have been instrumental in catapulting British speedway into one of the sport's most highly successful and significant eras in its history ... by getting himself banned.

And all that was before he forsook the English city of his birth, had half his brain removed (See below) and became a citizen of New Zealand. In Waitakere City actually, which is in Auckland.

He later admitted that his 'bottle had gone'. But let him explain the whole sorry business in his own words. How did it all start, Bob?

WELL, IT WAS LIKE THIS: I went to Harringay as a twelve-year-old, saw Vic Duggan and I wanted to do that. My first practice was at Rye House speedway track and the guy that put Jack Young on the map, Clem Mitchell, was running the training school. It cost £5 for 20 laps and that was probably more than my wages for a week. So I went there on Coronation Day, 2 June 1953. It was nice and quiet, with everyone watching their tellys and having street parties.

I was seventeen and you had to go in the army at eighteen to do two years National Service. So everyone said: 'Wait until you come out of the army.' But I thought I want to know if I will be able to do it, so I went and had five practices and Clem Mitchell said: 'You have a bit of talent so I'll send you to Wimbledon. They have a lot of overseas riders and want some English talent.'

I went to Plough Lane and I had no bike. I had a leather coat, jeans and some boots with no steel shoe and a helmet. When I got there Ronnie Greene, the promoter, asked what type of bike I had and I said I hadn't got a bike, so he said I could use the track spare which was Norman Parker's who was captain of Wimbledon and England. He'd had an accident the year before and that was virtually the end for him, but they still had his bike. They wanted £150 for it but I only had £50.

I was signed on without being looked at, just on the word of Clem Mitchell. Ronnie Greene said: 'Bring your Dad up here to sign a contract to say he'll pay me for the bike if you don't. I'll give you some rides, and out of any second half winnings you will pay for the bike.'

I broke a thumb in a race just before I went for my Army medical. So was grade 3, and had to go again later. Then I think I had some other accident and I was grade 3 again. Conscription was coming to an end so I never went in to the Army.

We were on concrete starts then, and they where a problem, especially when wet, so sometimes from my winnings I would be giving him 4s 6d (22.5pence) after insurance and a gallon of fuel, and that was it. The track manager was not keen to run me but Ronnie Greene would say, in his posh accent: 'Go on, give the boy a ride.'

The inspiration: Vic Duggan at Harringay ... Bob wanted to be like that.

I can remember going into the first corner and it was very slick, so I've gone down and ripped the arse out of my trousers and I was all red raw like. Barry Briggs and Ronnie Moore and all the others were laughing, and Ronnie Greene says: 'Get up and have another go lad.' Later Ronnie Moore said to me: 'We are having a practice here at 7am tomorrow.' Which was a problem for me with travelling 1½ hours across London to get there.

Ronnie Moore said: 'You can use my leathers and boots from the dressing room.' So I got into these leathers and in the pocket is a Cooper label because Ronnie was racing Cooper cars at the time. My girlfriend then was named Cooper so that label went in my pocket. Out to the track I waited on the bike, I had never started it up, you see, because at the training school they did that for you.

Ronnie Greene was over at the start line saying: 'Send the boy over, send the boy over.' So they push me and it's going bang, bang because I am trying to turn the throttle, but they sorted me out and started it for me. Then I said I had never done a start so they said: 'Just rev up and make more noise than all the other guys.'

When I got to the line on the concrete there was a space there and they called me up, and I remember *'make more noise than all the others'*, so I was going wham, wham, wham with the throttle. I had done cycle speedway and knew about tapes, and that you mustn't move, so my reactions were quick. The tape went up, I dropped the clutch and I was gone and I won that race first time out! There were three experienced riders in the race.

Ronnie Moore filmed it but I didn't see it because you were frightened to talk to Ronnie because he was like a God. I don't know if he's still got the film now. He was a great teacher and passed things on.

This was in 1954. In one second half ride they gave me at the end of the season it was pouring with rain. I gated well but went into the bend slow and all the others came past and put me in the fence. But I managed to keep running and managed to get up to second place and Ronnie Greene made a big thing of that and had me talk on the microphone. All I could say was: 'It's very wet out there tonight'. So after that I used to race regularly in the second half races.

I was a good gater, like Dave Gifford. When I got in the Wimbledon team I rode with Ronnie Moore and he would say: 'if you get to the corner first, leave a gap about a foot from the line and if I have to, I will come by. With Ronnie nursing me, I used to win races, but the next year they put me with Briggo and I would leave that hole on the line for him and he would come through and stick me straight into the fence.

Ronnie used to teach riders how to come out of a corner, and Briggo would tell them to go into the corner at a million miles an hour. It's like learning to fly when they teach you

So he went to Rye House to see if he could do it … and he could – but not quite well enough because Jimmy Gleed is being presented with the winner's trophy by Wembley star Tommy Price. Bob has obviously been behind most of the time.

But he got some rides with the California team in the Southern Area League, which was about as low as you could get in the Fifties. The team is, from the left: Manager Fred Millward, Peter Mould, Jimmy Gleed, Gil Goldfinch, Fred Babcock, Keith Webb, secretary G. Griffin. In front Bob, Ron Sharp on bike and George Baker.

At Wimbledon they didn't take him seriously at first, but eventually it began to come right and he helped the Dons win the league in 1959. Taking a celebratory tractor ride are, from left: Peter Moore, Ron How, Gerald Jackson, Gerry King, manager Ted Brine, Cyril Brine, Cyril Maidment and Ronnie Moore. Bob is the cheeky chappie with the little beard at the front. Straight-laced martinet promoter Ronnie Greene is in the suit and hat far left.

how to take off and when you're in the air they yell up at you: 'Next week I will teach you how to land.' It really is better to teach them to come in gentle, then slowly turn it on.

Briggo would say: 'You've got to go in quicker.' But I thought I don't want this, so I was going to give it all up, and then I went to South Africa to ride for Trevor Redmond. Before I went I bought a brand new chrome Rotrax bike. Briggo saw it and wanted to borrow it as a spare for the World Final. At World Finals, riders always put their spare bike out near the start line for the presentation.

It was nice to see my shiny new bike out there. When he gave it back he moaned like hell as he had to put a new clutch cable on it, but that was good because then the clutch worked better, and I think he charged me for it. *Ha! Ha!*

So I went to South Africa thinking that I would be a disaster because Ove Fundin was there, and Olle Nygren. Racing in Pretoria and around Johannesburg you are up high above sea level and it's like riding a 350cc, which was good for me because the power of a 500cc used to frighten me.

I could never screw it on like the others did, but I learned a bit of throttle control there because I could get away with less throttle on a slick track, and when we went to Durban back at sea level it was great as I was learning to cope with the full throttle and the power of a 500cc. They held the South African championship and I got third place. I finished higher than Ove Fundin.

Fundin never left the line, and when I out gated him – a couple of times at Wimbledon – I would ride a very narrow line all around the track and it felt good when I won. What I didn't like is afterwards they would leave their bike on the track and a mechanic would come out to push it into the pits. *(Making out they had trouble with the bike?)*

From there I started to move forward and began winning races back in England. Then it was 1959 and I started to score some points for Wimbledon, but I wasn't consistent enough. Then it got to 1960 and I got to the World Final as reserve. I had blown a motor up at the wrong time when leading a semi final round so was reserve for the Final. I had a ride and got a second. Next year I was in the first Final held outside England. It was held at Malmo in Sweden in 1961 and I got joint fifth there with Ronnie Moore. We had 10 points each. *(Bob actually finished one place higher because he beat Ronnie into second place in their last ride, Heat 18)*

In 1962 at Wembley I was joint fifth again. The next month my son was born and suddenly my focus was gone, he seemed to be more important than speedway, so I missed out on the 1963 Final. Then in 1964 I rode in my last World Final at Gothenburg in Sweden.

At the practice day most riders were on Jawas and I was still on a JAP, but I could outgate them so I thought I should be in the first half dozen on Final night, but it rained and rained so they put tons of sawdust on the track, and we thought it would be cancelled, but it wasn't because people had come from overseas.

Briggo was clued up. He rented a hotel room and went to bed in the afternoon so didn't see the rain and he arrived ready to win, which he did, with the Russian Igor Pletchenov second and Ove Fundin third. But if you got behind them with that bloody sawdust it was terrible. My first start was off gate four so I was behind two of them throwing up dirt. I weighed double my weight when I finished the race.

In 1963 Bob decided to make New Zealand his home. He says: 'They suggested I apply to become a Kiwi, so I had half my brain removed and became one. That allowed me to then race for New Zealand.'

At this time there was an unholy row going on within British speedway between the 'legitimate' National League and the recently formed pirate – or Black – Provincial League, which was doing better. Bob happened to catch a glimpse of Ivan Mauger's payslip. Ivan, who was riding for Provincial League Newcastle at the time, was getting about three times what Bob was getting with National League Wimbledon. So Bob threw in his lot with Provincial League renegade Mike Parker's Wolverhampton. He rode one match for the Wolves and was promptly served with a writ in the Hackney pits banning him. He says: 'I think jumping ship did help the formation of both leagues.' Soon afterwards the disagreement between the leagues was resolved by Lord Shawcross's Report, the warring factions amalgamated and British speedway was able to advance into the broad, sunlit uplands of a new British League in 1965 bringing with it one of the sport's most successful periods … until the later insidious advent of the World Championship Grands Prix.

Carry on Bob…

I was still racing every year in England, except 1966. I stayed in New Zealand and in the winter I won the North Island grass track championship, then went on to win the New Zealand national grass track title.

During the next few years I rode for New Zealand in Test matches and a combined team of English, New Zealand and Australian riders called Great Britain. Then in 1969 I had the racing experience but could not get the hang of the Jawa, so went back to a JAP engine in a Jawa frame. This gave me throttle control again. I'd missed that with the Jawa because they rev a lot. But if you're on a JAP they have the power low down.

Roy Trigg and I had the same set-up of a JAP in a Jawa frame. We were running lower gears with the JAPs than we used to, and we were getting a better meeting.

Ronnie Moore always used a lower gear because he said he could get out of the gate quicker, and throttle control was a bit better. We would have used it years before if we had listened to him.

There's a little story about Ronnie. I bought one of his 58 tooth back sprockets from one of his mechanics which had RM and 58 stamped on it. I already had a 59 sprocket, and I was told to always go down a tooth for the second half because the track gets slicker. I had a young cousin about fourteen who asked what the number 58 was on the side of the sprocket and I said it meant how many of those little spike things it had. But he said no it was 59. So we counted it and sure enough it was a 59 marked 58.

Ronnie would mark his sprockets with different numbers so that when other riders came along to spy on his bike they would get the wrong information. So here I was for a whole

Bob says he doesn't remember this. It was at the British Final of the World Championship in 1968. He says: 'Was it me? Or did I get concussion?' He got concussion … which is probably why he didn't remember it.

season changing my gear and wondering why my chain length didn't alter. I was no good at this stuff and used to pay people to do my bike. I could do the tyre pressures.

As I got older and got more experience I had some good meetings and that's when I was put in that World's Best Pairs as the New Zealand team with Ivan Mauger which we won in Stockholm in 1969. Briggo would not race in Sweden that year. He had an argument with the Swedes over something or other *(he claimed they had libelled him)* so he said he wouldn't ride there any more.

I wasn't going to go to the World Pairs thing because my bike and gear was all packed ready to go to New Zealand. But the officials said that if I didn't go I wouldn't be allowed to ride in New Zealand.

There was a Test match at Malmo and I was reserve for this match. Then next day I flew up to Stockholm with Ivan Mauger. We shared a hotel room and talked about our cycle speedway days, and the fact that he wanted to be one of the best dressed people in Britain, which I thought strange. We also talked about our early days at Wimbledon, when Ivan was a groundsman. After meetings I would wait for him to tidy up the showers then I would give him a lift home. They were good old days.

He wasn't a bad bloke back then. But the 'Pom' in me later used to take the piss and he couldn't take it. Briggo could, and gave it back in kind. But I have mates in speedway who the more you take the piss the greater that friend is. And I love it when I get it back.

Like for example when I told you I was inducted into The (New Zealand) Hall of Fame you said: 'They must be scraping the barrel.' Now that is what a close friend would say,

Ah, but then he did get good enough to win a trophy, and here he is looking rather pleased with himself – and why not – on the receiving end.

Eventually he became good enough to reach a World Championship Final, it was his second, in 1961 at Malmo in Sweden. The happy band are, from the left, standing: Ronnie Moore, Ray Cresp, Barry Briggs, Bjorn Knutsson, Ove Fundin, Mike Broadbank, Ken McKinlay, Rune Sormander, Florian Kapala, Leif Larsson, Gote Nordin and Ron How. Kneeling: Stanlislaw Tkocz, Cyril Maidment, Jack Young, Bob, Igor Plechanov and Peter Craven. Bob finished fifth with ten points.

Made it: Bob gets mixed up with the real elite – all world champions … except him. He is on the outside, Peter Craven leads from Barry Briggs with Ronnie Moore at the back.

Above left: *The last World Final … Gothenburg 1964 in the rain. They thought it would be called off, but it wasn't and everyone is all nice and clean because they haven't yet been out to plough through the sodden sawdust. The British contingent taking cover under a makeshift umbrella are Cyril Maidment, Barry Briggs, Mike Broadbank and Dick Fisher. Bob goes it alone and Nigel Boocock uses his helmet.*

Above right: *Presentation time at the British League Riders Championship Final at West Ham in 1965 and Tommy Price introduces Olympic athlete Mary Rand to the riders. Ken McKinlay is first and Bob flashes her a smile waiting for his turn while Nigel Boocock finds it all rather amusing.*

so I loved it. I had been out to Australia in the Test team in 1959/60 and to New Zealand as a freelance rider in 1962 and wanted to live there. On those earlier trips I had done well as I was a gater and could win from the front. But on handicaps, sometimes 130 yards back and only three laps, I still won but I learned a lot about passing being that far back.

So it helped me back in the UK. Some English riders said I wouldn't like it in New Zealand as they pay funny rates for winning, but as it happened I got paid a guaranteed amount, and had to put on a bit of a show like not passing too early but make exciting racing out of it.

I was riding regularly in New Zealand and was appearing at Templeton and Western Springs until 1972. Then, just before Christmas 1973, I broke my back at Western Springs. I returned to the track later but I was just riding and not really racing, not rushing through and making gaps, because my bottle had gone. But they were paying me good money and I wanted my son to ride, so I kept going but he didn't want to ride. So that was that.

You can tell what a crowd-puller Bob was by the state of the terraces as he leads Charlie Monk at Glasgow.

I never hated anyone in speedway, or vowed revenge on them. If I was fenced or pushed over I would just remember it and maybe close a gap on them later, but I was never accused of being dirty. In fact many said if I could get a cruel streak I would have been a better rider.

Fame at last ... Bob with the plaque proclaiming he has been honoured by being inducted into the New Zealand Speedway Hall Of Fame.

Nothing daunted ... you can't keep a good chap down. Keep smiling, that was Bob's motto, but did he post that sign behind him as a warning to the opposition ... or was it to deter any lurking jobsworth with a banning writ?

Bob's racing career spanned eighteen years during which he rode for California, Wimbledon, Wolverhampton, Cradley and Hackney. As well as the World Pairs title he won with Ivan Mauger in 1969, there were 33 international appearances for England and Great Britain and 27 for New Zealand, five league championships with Wimbledon and he has four National Trophy winner's medals. He now does exhibition races and even rode in his seventy-first year. He also runs regular schools for solo riders.

Alec Statham

THE CASE OF THE MISSING GRAND PIANO

AN EXTREMELY INTERESTING ITEM came my way not all that long ago. It was totally unexpected, but it was something I had been seeking for some considerable time.

And it enabled me to lay the ghost of Alec Statham.

This obviously calls for a little explanation.

It has been my never-ending quest to seek out information and report on the careers of the legendary speedway heroes of my formative years. So I was incredulous to be told a piece of somewhat startling incidental speedway intelligence. It was this: that Alec Statham had been observed enjoying a pint of good English ale in a public house in Hinckley, Leicestershire.

Incredulous because Alec would be celebrating his 103rd birthday this year. The words 'would be' are very carefully and deliberately chosen because, though there is a record of Alec's birth, 30 May 1912 at Keresley, a village within the parish of Coventry in Warwickshire, at the time there was – curiously – no record of his death. At least, not one that I had been able to find.

Even after a painstaking search through the speedway archives, and a diligent trawl across the modern Internet, the road always ended in a total blank … with no notice of Alec's demise.

A hundred and three, you say? Well, why not? Canadian star Jimmy Gibb, West Ham, Wimbledon; catchphrase: Never Gibb Up – celebrated his 102nd birthday only a couple of years ago.

So, I had all but given up on the question of unravelling the mystery of the supposed sighting of Alec Statham, when … out of the blue came …

Starting out, a young Alec Statham at the beginning of his career at Harringay among some of the biggest personalities in the sport. Not everyone is identifiable, but those taking a front row seat are, from the left: Promoter Tom Bradbury-Pratt, Bill Pitcher, Billy Dallison, Jack Ormston, Jack Parker, Phil Bishop – the modest Alec is standing right behind him – Les Wotton, Norman Parker, Charles Knott also a promoter. Significantly, standing at the back slightly taller than the others fourth from the left is 'Wizard' Frank Arthur, one of the original Australian pioneers who introduced the sport to Britain in 1928.

… But no, I think I'll save just what it was until later.

Because you should know that when it came to speedway style, there was no one to come within touching distance of Alec Statham. Alec was the epitome of style. Only America's Wilbur Lamoreaux could demonstrate anything near the Statham elegance on a bike.

Alec Statham, as well as being acknowledged as one of the greatest and smoothest operators on the track, was one of the quiet men of speedway – a pipe-smoking nice guy who never went out of his way to court publicity. But in the assessment of his long-time friend, sometime captain, team mate and occasional opponent, Norman Parker, Alec Statham was world class and undoubtedly one of England's finest.

Yet, said Norman: 'No matter what Alec did, things had a habit of getting up and biting him'. Even to the tragic loss of his prized grand piano … an explanation for which will also be revealed in due course.

Alec Statham's star rose to its zenith in the speedway firmament when full time league racing resumed just after the war in 1946. The days were dim, dark and austerity-ridden.

Speedway promoters who had survived the conflict had very little to do except count the money being poured into their apparently bottomless coffers by the millions – yes, that's correct, millions – of entertainment-starved sports fans who were flocking to the twelve tracks in the two sections, the six tracks in the National (First Division) League and the further six in the Northern (Second Division) League.

Alec wearing the distinctive Harringay Tigers jersey.

Compared with what we have today that's not very many. Why did the fans keep cramming the terraces week after week to watch the same teams over and over again? They turned up – Wembley and Wimbledon were known to have had to close their gates and lock out thousands for even ordinary league matches, let alone World Finals – because the racing was fabulous, that's why.

And at the time there was precious little to distract the war-weary populace in the way of alternative entertainment and thrills, and at the same time even less to attract the big time pre-war overseas stars back to Britain where practically everything was still rationed.

And therefore box office top draws, such as Australia's Lionel Van Praag, Max Grosskreutz and Vic and Ray Duggan, as well as America's Jack and Cordy Milne, decided conditions were too spartan and chose to stay at home in their respective lands of plenty.

Once more, Britain stood alone – well, in the world of league speedway it did.

To my way of thinking, the way things were at the time the promoters could easily have afforded to have got together and hired an exclusive ocean liner to bring all the big boys back to Blighty and put each one up in a personal suite at The Ritz hotel. Still, as they were chuckling all the way to their banks without really trying … what was the point of trying? So, as far as speedway was concerned, they did what the authorities did with the bread and butter and meat and eggs and sweets and coal and clothing and petrol. They rationed out the riches.

The real National League riches were the six survivors whose pre-war performances designated them as Stars. And one went to each of the top teams: Norman Parker went to Wimbledon, Eric Chitty went to West Ham, Ron Johnson went to New Cross, Bill Kitchen went to Wembley, Jack Parker went to Belle Vue and – this is where Alec Statham came in – Alec went to Odsal Bradford. To begin with, as Grade One talent, they qualified for £1.50 a start and £1.75 a point – in today's money that was almost £36.50 a start and £42.50 a point.

The race card of the wartime Belle Vue Bulletin for 27 April 1940. At the time this Belle Vue v Harringay meeting was going on British troops were pulling out of Norway ahead of the German invasion and Himmler was setting up the concentration camp at Auschwitz.

What remained of the lesser talent was pooled to equalise all team strengths. That was the theory anyway. And they were paid less of course.

An early biographer had concluded that speedway was Alec Statham's destiny, and there has not yet been a man born who has been able to thumb his nose at destiny. It certainly seemed that way for Alec.

World class he undoubtedly was, inarguably a major talent, though rather like the glamorous Australian pioneer idol of the Old Kent Road faithful, Ron Johnson, he never quite managed to win the meetings, or titles, that made reporters want to write the word 'great' before his name. Even though there were the World Finals, before and after the war, a considerable number of appearances for England, at home and in Australia, and he was nominated for two cracks at Jack Parker's British Match Race Championship.

Yet Alec Statham may well be primarily remembered because he was the first speedway rider to be transferred for the astounding sum of £2,000 when he moved to Wimbledon in 1948. It was a fee that, at the time, was thought to be the ceiling price beyond which no sane promoter would dare to go. And even more astounding, Alec was then fast approaching his 36th birthday.

His birthplace was close by the home of the British motorcycle industry, and as a young man speedway attracted him. Trials at Brandon soon won him a place in the Coventry team, and as he progressed he moved to Birmingham and then Southampton.

By the mid-Thirties Alec, a good businessman, had his own successful garage, which began to take up more and more of his time. Speedway became little more than a hobby and, according to Norman Parker, this attitude may have been why the sport's major prizes eluded him.

'Alec was a sportsman,' said Norman. 'He rode speedway for the love of it, really. We all did – Jack, Alec and me. We honestly didn't make a fabulous living at it. It didn't matter enough to Alec, yet if you wound him up enough he was unbeatable.'

So Alec quit racing and the bright lights, reportedly to concentrate on his business interests, though there were suggestions that he thought he was not really good enough to reach the very top.

But in 1937, after a crisis in his business life, Harringay chief Tom Bradbury-Pratt tempted him back into leathers and Alec became a member of the fabulous Harringay Tigers team that was a top attraction right up to the war.

The side included the Parker brothers, Jack Ormston, Billy Dallison, Bill Pitcher, Dick Harris, Les Wotton and Lloyd Goffe. It was during this period that Alec emerged as a genuine international star, forcing his way into the England team and qualifying for the 1937, 1938 and 1939 World Finals.

Norman Parker reckoned that he and Alec were the two best team riders in the sport – aside from his England partnership with brother Jack – and it was with Alec that in 1939 they first developed the speedway dirt deflector, now as universal as the silencer on modern speedway machines.

Decades before the accepted modern version of the dirt deflector was perfected, a remarkably similar Statham-Parker pre-war contraption was tested by the pair at Harringay. It looked virtually the same as is universally mandatary today yet, according to Norman, it was 'completely useless, but great for publicity'.

When it came to team riding, Norman admitted that even big time First Division stars could get their comeuppance on the track. He remembered an early post-war meeting at Second Division Newcastle when the pair of them had became team mates again at Wimbledon. He said: 'Alec and I were all set to show them what invincible team riding was all about. Instead, we both fell off at the first bend like a couple of novices. We were the ones who were shown up.'

When war came Alec set up a factory in Coventry to produce military components and he continued to race in the famous weekly wartime meetings at Belle Vue. His best year was 1945 when he won the Northern Championship and the All England Best Pairs with Ron Johnson. And he was one of the ENSA team of riders who toured the Continent entertaining the troops in Occupied Europe.

Alec's wartime enterprise was very successful, Norman Parker said: 'He did quite well for himself, rather fancying himself as a man of means, getting himself a super flat, installing a grand piano and even learning how to play it.'

It was ironic that Alec's marriage later broke up and his wife went to live in America, which was when he lost his prized grand piano. She took it with her.

When a full programme of league racing resumed after the war, as a top performer Alec continued his career at international level. Test matches against Australia were resumed in 1947 and his appearance in the opener before a crowd of 47,050 on what was then his home track, Odsal, was probably his best for England, though there had been doubts about him taking part because of injury.

Alec did ride, with seven stitches in a serious head wound, and in the 65 – 43 England victory his score of 16, which included one precarious win with a broken front fork, was matched only by team mate Bill Kitchen and Australia's brilliant Vic Duggan.

But Alec's – almost – finest hour was to come the following year at Wembley in the World Championship substitute, the Speedway Riders Championship Final. Vic Duggan's phenomenal form had dominated speedway since he had returned to Britain the previous year. Alec was the only rider to beat Duggan in the Final. They had met in their first rides, Heat 4, and indeed it looked to be Alec's title after four unbeaten rides.

His final two rides were in Heats 16 and 17. The 85,000 crowd at Wembley were unaware that he was riding with a knee injury, and afterwards Alec admitted that had it been an ordinary league match he would not have considered riding.

Perhaps the strain of taking on Oliver Hart, Lloyd Goffe and Wilbur Lamoreaux in Heat 16, had taken its toll and two rides in succession was too much.

I was at Wembley that night, and the way I saw it from the terraces was that Alec lifted at the start of Heat 16 and it took him two laps to get past Lloyd Goffe and Wilbur Lamoreaux. Oliver Hart, who was leading, was fully aware that he had no chance of winning the meeting but Alec did so, in what can only be described as a magnanimous gesture, he moved over on the last bend and allowed Alec to go past, gifting him the three points in what was reported as 'the most thrilling race of the meeting … '.

Prince Philip, who presented the winner's trophy, was extremely unimpressed by what he had seen, according to reliable sources, and it is significant that he has never attended another speedway meeting.

But whether or not Oliver Hart was indeed being generous to a former team mate, it was all in vain. Out in the following race when he could have wrapped up the title, Alec

The accommodation was not exactly five-star for members of the ENSA touring team when they entertained the occupying forces in Europe during the winter of 1945-46. Alec uses his Army issue greatcoat to keep warm.

Star turn: Alec leads the Bradford team when full time league racing resumed in 1946. Standing at the back from the left are: Albert Rosenfeld, Vic Pitcher, Ernie Price, Jack Tye, Ron Clarke, Bill Longley and Fred Tuck. Promoter Johnnie Hoskins has hitched a ride on Alec's bike.

Above left:
Consulting the
captain in the pits:
Ron Clarke, left, and
Fred Tuck look to
Alec, centre, for
advice. Albert
Rosenfeld is far
right, and listening
in is visiting West
Ham skipper Eric
Chitty.

Above right: Neat
and tidy, that was
Alec. The epitome of
style out front and
no one within
touching distance.

finished third behind Bill Longley and Split Waterman, going on to lose a run-off for second place to Ron Johnson.

Duggan clinched the title two races later by winning Heat 19 and putting him on an unassailable total of 14. A second place for Alec in Heat 17 would have put him in a run-off for the championship with Duggan. As it was, when Ron Johnson won the final heat to finish on 13 points, the same score as Alec's, it meant a run-off with the New Cross captain for the minor rostrum places. And Johnson won that to take second place.

In what can only be described as a painful anti-climax, Alec had been on the brink of true greatness only to have to face failure within the space of four races.

Speedway historians constantly recall the melodramatic climax of the 1951 World Final when an identical set of circumstances doomed the chances of Australia's Jack Biggs, in a meeting that has come to be remembered more as the World Final that Jack Biggs lost rather than the World Final that was sensationally won by a Second Division rider, Jack Young, who was then with Edinburgh.

In the event, beneath the headline 'Alec Statham Stole The Show', reporters sought an explanation for Alec letting the title slip away so dramatically. He told them: 'Perhaps I was shaken by rearing in the previous heat. Longley and Waterman were not going so very fast that I should have been incapable of overhauling them. Yet I just couldn't make it.' One commentator wrote: 'It was typical of the gallant Statham, sportsman that he is, that he refused to offer an excuse.'

Alec was ranked sixth in the world after his performance and when 1949 came around and the official World Championship was revived, the commentators were looking to Alec to be the first Englishman to take the crown. But he qualified only as a reserve for the Final.

Though on Wimbledon's retained list for the 1952 season, Alec called it a day. New and

Left: Alec, for an astounding record £2,000 transfer fee, joined Wimbledon in 1948: From left, Lionel Levy, Archie Windmill (who was tall), Alec (who wasn't), promoter Ronnie Greene, George Saunders, Dennis Gray, Les Wotton, Dick Harris, Mike Erskine and Cyril Brine. Norman Parker is on the bike.

Right: The one that got away – and aboard the Wembley tractor Alec seems to be looking for it; his almost finest hour at the 1948 Speedway Riders Championship Final. He seemed to have it won and, on the brink of true greatness, he let it slip. Vic Duggan has the winner's trophy and Ron Johnson won the run-off with Alec to even deny him second place.

brilliant talents such as Ronnie Moore had arrived to blaze the trail for a new speedway generation.

They called Alec 'The Stylist Of Them All'. In his own special quiet way, he may well have taken an extra contemplatory puff on his ubiquitous pipe and considered that to have been a more acceptable accolade than Speedway Champion Of The World.

But, you know, I am still wondering who that 'Alec Statham' was seen enjoying a pint of good old English ale in that Hinckley pub. Because, as I revealed earlier, quite out of the blue one of my correspondents, Alan Barwick, sent me a photograph of Alec's gravestone.

His accompanying letter read:

I have carried out some further research on Alec Statham which I have attached. Reports of a sighting of Alec propping up the bar in Hinckley recently sadly could not be true, unless it was a ghostly apparition, because Alec died of a cerebral haemorrhage at the Hospital of St Cross in Rugby on 8 March 1977, and his body was cremated.

His home address was Rafters, Bourton-on-Dunsmore, which is a small rural village south-east of Coventry.

Alec was chairman/managing director of his company, Alec Statham Ltd, which was located in Brandon Road, Binley, Coventry.

His first wife was Doreen May Evans. They married at Meriden, Warwickshire in 1936 and she went with him on his trips to Australia in 1938 and 1939. They separated during the war, and in 1946 she married an American GI.

It appears that Alec remarried a Ruby L. Crowhurst in 1951 who died in Coventry in 1964. It does not appear that Alec had any children, and the informant on his death certificate was a Peter Chamberlain.

Regards,
Alan Barwick

It was all so close … the influential speedway Press was contemplating whether Alec's rightful place was as England's number one.

The spirit of Alec Statham lies here … and the ghost is laid to rest.

John Chaplin writes: I am most grateful to Alan for the information on Alec Statham. A number of people had been in touch to tell me they knew that Alec had really died. But Alan has filled in a great deal of detail not only about when, where and how Alec died but also about his life away from speedway. The question of whether it was really Alec in that Hinckley pub, one of speedway's various apparitions (which have always intrigued me) or whether it was merely an Alec Statham lookalike had puzzled me for years. Now, of course, thanks to Alan, we have at last laid the ghost.

Ron Johnston

JOHNNO THE NAUGHTY NEW ZEALANDER

NEW ZEALAND IS STEEPED in speedway history, folklore … and fabulous success. It was a relative outpost in the global concept of the sport until recent years when the first Grand Prix of the year began to be held there.

The country's population today is put at only a fraction over 4,500,000 compared with Britain's 61,000,000 and America's near 320,000,000.

It is about as far away from recognized civilization as it is possible to get on this planet, which is why it was one of the last major landmasses to be settled by humans, somewhere around the middle of the 13th century.

So what its knights of the speedway track have accomplished in the intervening eight centuries – they couldn't have even had the wheel is long as the rest of us – in winning a round dozen World Championships is quite a remarkable achievement.

In speedway terms it means that in the seventy-nine years since the World Championship was first introduced, New Zealanders merit an overall bronze medal. They have earned a place on the metaphorical championship rostrum with Sweden and Denmark who have won 14 World titles each.

Of course, you have to remember that the man who always claimed to have started the whole thing, Mr Johnnie Stark Hoskins, also came from New Zealand. He was born in Waitara in the Taranaki Region of the North island in 1892.

Do you wonder where all this is going? Well, let me throw the names of a few New Zealand speedway champions at you: Charlie Blacklock, Wally Kilmister, Dick Campbell, Harold Fairhurst, Jackie Hunt, Bruce Abernethy, Trevor Redmond, Geoff Mardon, Larry Ross, Maury Dunn, Merv Neil, Mitch Shirra, Bruce Cribb and Charlie Tonks.

The name Charlie Tonks will surely be unfamiliar, but the records show that he did ride for New Zealand. And there is not only London-born Bob Andrews (who emigrated to New Zealand and has insisted 'I had to have half my brain removed' to qualify him to captain the NZ national team – but also the ultra-talented trio who really need no introduction at all: Moore, Mauger and Briggs.

Apart from them, our other true Kiwi legend is someone whose prodigious talent has for far too long been overshadowed by the higher profile of Peter Craven, as well as those other World Champions from New Zealand. The name is Ron Johnston. That's *Johnston with a T*. For a solid eleven years round the old Belle Vue track at Hyde Road you tangled with Johnno at your peril.

No less a person than Ove Fundin, five-times a World title holder, remembers him well. Ove says: 'Ron was a very good rider and a very hard one. But I got the impression he didn't much care for foreigners. I was a foreigner and of course the Australians and the New Zealanders at the time didn't think of themselves as foreigners.'

Bob Andrews, no mean performer himself with a world ranking of No.5 in 1961, is of a similar opinion. He says: 'Ron was a hard man around Belle Vue. We had a four-lap race there once where we were shoulder to shoulder all the way. A nudge here and a nudge there. Ken Sharples said afterwards that it was one of the best races he had ever seen.'

Ron says: 'I always enjoyed riding against Ove. I didn't consider my self as a foreigner because my mother and father came from Scotland. Ove was a very good clean rider and we got on well together. One year after the English season finished I was in Sweden and he helped me buy a watch for my wife Josie. He got the owner of the shop to sell it to me for £50. She still wears it today and it is insured for six hundred and fifty NZ dollars (£332) … so, thanks Ove.

'As far as being hard is concerned, I admit I never used to put up with any nonsense around Belle Vue. I always gave as good as I got. Jack Parker taught me never to do anything hasty and to 'always remember there will always be a time when you can get your own back.'

Ron Johnston was born at Norwood Street, North East Valley, a suburb of Dunedin on the South island of New Zealand, on 31 December, 1930. He says: 'My mother told me I was born just after 11pm, and if I'd have been born an hour later, I'd have been a year younger.'

Originally from Scotland his parents emigrated to New Zealand. Ron remembers: 'My father's brother used to look after Robbie Burns's cottage near Dumfries.' Unlike New

Partners … the immaculate Jack Parker 'looking after' a slightly untidy Ron on the inside with Wembley's Fred Williams anxiously seeking an opening at the back.

Cross idol Ron Johnson, also of Scottish origin, who dropped the 'T' from his name when he was taken to Australia as a child, the Johnstons held on to their 'T'.

Ron was a farmer's boy. He says: 'Those were good days. I was always up early in my younger days, about 4.30am; we had to get the milk run done early.

'Most of the family, my sisters, usually went to church on a Sunday. My brother Tom and I in those days would get on the bus to town, but we wouldn't go to church. We'd walk home, to spend the bus money on lollies.'

He left school at 15 and wanted to buy a motorcycle, though at that time he hadn't a clue what speedway was. He says: 'I don't know why I wanted a motorbike – it was the thing to do, I think. I had enough money to buy an old side-valve Triumph, which wasn't very fast'

He wanted something better, and with one of his friends, Robert Booth – 'we used to call him The Ferret; I don't know why we called him that' – decided to save up and buy a new bike each.

They got jobs at a meat freezing factory. 'We worked from six in the morning until seven at night,' says Ron. 'I was given the job of cutting the sheep in half. We ordered our motorbikes – of course in those days you couldn't buy anything off the shelf, so we had to wait 18 months. We ordered them with a single exhaust pipe, and these bikes came with twin pipes, so sooner than wait another 18 months for delivery we accepted the bikes with twin exhaust pipes. I'd made enough money to pay for mine, it was an Ariel 500.

'I took up grass track racing, beach racing, road racing and hill climbs. I used to ride against Burt Munro on the beach.'

Munro was a champion New Zealand motorcycle racer famous for setting an under-1,000 cc world record at Bonneville on 26 August 1967. The 2005 film, *The Fastest Indian*, was based on Burt's exploits on his Indian motorcycle with Sir Anthony Hopkins playing Burt.

Ron remembers: 'Quite often we beat him, usually because his bike broke down or we wouldn't have done. We were only doing 110 miles an hour. He'd have been doing a lot faster when he was going. Us motorbike boys we used to be daredevils, we used to be naughty. In those days the police had Ford cars, and they weren't very fast – they could never catch us.

'Then we did some road racing near Christchurch. The speedway had started up there. We didn't know what speedway was, and we thought: boy oh boy, this is good!

'Back in Dunedin we heard that there was a track at Tahuna Park opening up, so I decided to sell my Ariel and buy a speedway bike. It had a Max Grosskreutz frame with a 500 JAP engine, and of course there were no brakes or anything like that on it.

'The directors found out that Jack Parker and Ron Mason, speedway riders from Belle Vue in England, were riding in Australia, and they invited them over to teach us how to ride. We thought Jack Parker was World Champion. Every day we'd practice – and Ron was trying to teach us. He said: "Ride around here, to me, ride four laps flat out without turning the throttle off." Which I did, quite easily really I suppose. In those days I was a daredevil.

'Ron Mason taught us everything he knew, we didn't take it all in, as you can imagine, but I did quite well, and I won the South Island Championship that year. At the end of the season Ron got on the microphone to the crowd and said: "Send this boy to England, and I'll look after him".

'That was me. The crowd took up a collection – I think they collected £115 – it was a lot of money in those days. The promoters did everything for me, they bought me a boat ticket to England, it took five weeks to get there. I was excited to be going, and scared as well, because I'd only ever been out of Dunedin as far as Christchurch. The family were all for it because it was an opportunity. I don't remember much about the trip, there were games and fancy dress and that. I didn't get seasick or anything.'

In England he was met in Southampton by fellow New Zealanders Bob McFarlane and Frank Boyle. Ron remembers: 'They had arrived a year before and rode for Oxford. On the Saturday they took me to Belle Vue, a big speedway centre near Manchester. Alice Hart was running the speedway, she also ran Sheffield. On the Sunday I had to prove that I was good enough to be signed up. I did well in the practice on the Sunday, and at that particular time you were only allowed to have two overseas riders per track, so she sent me to Belfast to the new track at Dunmore Park. I rode there for a little while and did quite well.

'Jack Chignell, an Australian, he got hurt at Sheffield, so Miss Hart pulled me out of Belfast, and put me in Sheffield to replace him. I rode for Sheffield for a while and won the Cussons Memorial Trophy.'

His performances for Sheffield – shattering the Plymouth track record on only his third appearance – attracted attention. It got him an almost instant switch back to Belle Vue.

Ron says: 'At Belle Vue there was a man called Charlie 'Pee Wee' Cullum, an American. He got hurt, so I went from Sheffield to Belle Vue. I stayed there for the rest of the time at speedway, eleven years.

'I was Jack Parker's partner for about three years. It was First Division. Jack was very good, he would look after me on the inside, he was fast. If he wanted me to go a bit faster he would creep along on the inside and push me on a bit, which I learned very well later on at every speedway.

'I got on very well with Jack Parker. I think he was the greatest rider of the lot. I used to do what he told me to do. I never rode with Peter Craven as his partner. He was a good rider but very moody. He didn`t like me beating him. I think Belle Vue was one of the best tracks, it was fair to all. I did very well there.

'In 1952 I won the New Zealand Championship, against good riders like Ronnie Moore and Bruce Abernethy. Ronnie and I decided that we'd fly back to England instead of going by boat, but it still took about four or five days. We called in at California and stayed with Jack and Cordy Milne and Ernie Roccio for a couple of days then we went on to New York. We went up the Empire State Building and took pictures and all that sort of stuff. It was all very fast and up to date really.

'Back in England In 1952 I used to stay at the garage with Ron Mason, and there was a girl in the office called Josie Wood. She was special. When I went home in 1953 I asked Josie to come with me. Of course by this time we were engaged. We got married, on 31 January 1953, in Dunedin, at Moray Place Congregational Church. We've been married now for more than sixty years. She's been a lovely wife.'

Ron had rapidly established himself as a rider of quality, and as the Aces third heat leader was rivalling Parker and Sharples. By 1953 he had bettered Parker, whose distinguished career was winding down, and by the following year he was the number one Ace, even outscoring Craven. And he reached his first World Final in 1955.

Ron says he doesn't remember the 1955 World Final. But the forecasters considered him the 'best outsider' with Cyril Roger and Arthur Wright. The pre-Final opinion was: 'You'd be surprised what this Kiwi can do when he really puts his mind to it.'

It was also predicted that 'the Swedes were out to clean up' and that Peter Craven would finish 'down the field'.

They were wrong on all three …

Taking a liberty: The 'special' office girl Josie Wood has a bit of a surprise when Ron gives her a public demonstration of appreciation … which turned out to be mutually satisfying because they got married the year after they met.

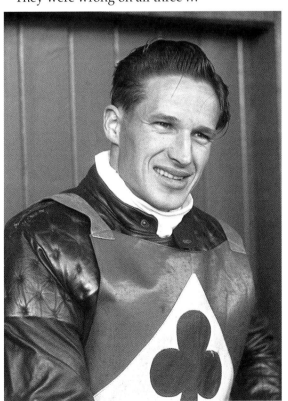

In Ron's first ride, Heat 2, he was matched against the new emperor of Hyde Road, his illustrious team mate Craven who had taken over as Belle Vue's top scorer, and Ove Fundin. He couldn't catch either of them, but he did pinch the third place point off Olle Nygren. And in the end it turned out to be Craven's night.

Another third place in Heat 7 behind Arthur Wright and Kjell Carlsson was followed In Heat 12 with a second place behind Arthur Forrest. Straight out again in the next heat it turned into a major drama with Brian Crutcher down and out on the first turn. In the re-run Eric Williams got the better of Barry Briggs and Ron had to be content with another third place.

Briggs and Williams were to meet again in an infamous three-man run-off scramble for the second and third rostrum places with Ronnie Moore.

The Ace ready to race: Ron in the Belle Vue pits before a meeting.

Three stars all set to shine before the 1960 World Final at Wembley, and two of them did: it was Ron's last Final, and his best, he finished in fifth place, one below Peter Moore on the right. But double World Champion Jack Young, centre, didn't shine at all that night, finishing way down in tenth place with a mere six points. The title went to Ove Fundin for a second time.

Up to no good: It looks as though Ron and Peter Craven have been having a torrid time of it on the track, so they have decided to set fire to manager Johnnie Hoskins's hat ... which was a fairly frequent occurrence ... and parade before the crowd. Ron has the can of fuel to keep the blaze going.

Ron joins the New Zealand international team strong enough to take on the might of England, though they did lose the series 3 - 0. The line-up is, standing from the left Maury Dunn, Goff Mardon, Ron, Barry Briggs. Front: Merv Neil, Trevor Redmond, Ronnie Moore and Peter Clark.

Moore settled it convincingly but Williams and Briggs controversially crashed on the last turn and Briggs rode side-saddle over the line for third. Williams was unable to get his bike going and confidently expected Briggs to be excluded for allegedly bringing him down … but he was disappointed.

Ron's final ride on Heat 18 had him up against Moore and Young. Moore's win over Young put him in that run-off and Ron's single point gave him a grand total of six, which meant tenth place overall.

Ron had to wait two years before getting another crack at the title. Eric Linden reported in *Speedway Star & News* that Johnston 'started well' with a Heat 4 win over Bob Roger, Ron How and Aage Hansen. Out again in the following heat, he dropped a point to veteran Aub Lawson.

His third ride was in Heat 12, and Linden's account of the race was: 'Briggs went out of the gate like a rocket and left the rest to sort it out.' The 'rest' were Fundin, Josef Hofmeister and Ron. Linden went on: 'Fundin was last out of the first turn but whipped past Hofmeister like he wasn't there, caught Johnston on the third lap and took another lap to pass him – and that seemed to knock the heart out of Ron.'

Parker couldn't resist giving Ron a helping hand. Long after he had retired from the track, old maestro Jack takes charge of warming up Ron's bike.

What Linden could not have known was what had gone on in the pits. Ron says: 'Barry had asked me to help him win the race as one New Zealander to another. I got out of the gate ahead of Ove Fundin and stopped him from getting past while Briggs went on to win. I was very naughty as I liked Ove Fundin. He was one of the top riders at the time. And a good chap.'

Ove Fundin remembers the race but, asked if he had words with Ron afterwards he says: 'No. I didn't feel all that sure of myself at the time. And in any case, it doesn't do any good after the referee has made his decision. It doesn't do yourself any good either because it unsettles you.'

Ron says he also doesn't remember the 1958 World Final. But he might like to know that he was picked by Johnnie Hoskins to finish third, with Craven to win and Fundin second.

Speedway Star columnists Danny Carter and Rick Eldon (guess who Rick Eldon **really** was) said they thought Ron had had a better chance the previous year 'but didn't make the most of it'. They said his form was good but Craven had to be beaten at Wembley and 'keeping up with Peter Craven was no easy task'.

That proved accurate when Ron lost to Craven and Ken McKinlay in his second rode. It was not until his fourth, in Heat 13, that he got a win over Ron How, Josef Hofmeister and Joel Jansson. He dropped another point to Aub Lawson in his final ride in Heat 18 to finish eighth overall. It was Lawson's best year. He finished third behind Briggs and Fundin.

Ron says: 'I did no preparation for a World Final, I treated it as just another meeting. I was a bit nervous about the crowd but it did not worry me too much. A lot of riders were very nervous.'

Nevertheless, he qualified for his fourth and last Final in 1960. The pre-meeting analysis said: 'He never seems to show his best form at World Finals. While he has all the know-how for the big occasion, the question is: can he convince himself he can ride Wembley?' It turned out to be his best and he finished fifth on ten points.

The reason, he says, he made no preparation for a World Final was because he was always too busy with the transport company that began to occupy his time from 1953. It was then that Ron's business and entrepreneurial skills had begun to show themselves – and undoubtedly distract him from the very highest success on the speedway track.

He began buying English cars to take back to New Zealand 'so we could make a bit of money. At that time the government charged 1s.9d in the pound tax on what I earned, and of course they used to include my English earnings. So I thought, well this is no good – it cost me a lot of money'.

Then the man who had first encouraged him to try his luck in England, Ron Mason – always a mediocre speedway rider at the best of times – was a successful haulage contractor and talked Ron into staying in England, buying a truck and working for him as an owner driver.

Boys just want to have fun: Ron, having succeeded as the Belle Vue captain, clowns for the camera with the aid of Peter Craven, Dick Fisher and Tink Maynard. Stan Ford is the driver.

Ron says: 'When the speedway season started I hired a man to drive my truck while I was riding. It was hard work running a business and riding speedway at the same time. We were riding several times a week sometimes.'

But it was the start of a successful business career that continued when he retired back home in New Zealand. And, after a chance meeting in a Dublin pub, Ron Mason went on

The established top-liner: Ron gets the better of Ronnie Moore.

Off to Poland in 1955, the first British team to go there after the war. Boarding are, from the top: Harold Jackson, Peter Craven, Arthur Wright, Ron, Ken Sharples, Fred Rogers, Dick Fisher, Peter Williams, Bob Duckworth, promoter Jack Fearnley and manager Johnnie Hoskins who held on to his hat.

to carve out another far more successful career as a racehorse owner.

Belle Vue was the first speedway team to go to Poland after the war. Ron says: 'It took us quite a long time to get there, we had to fly the bikes over. We were met by a Russian as we got off the plane. Of course we all got our cameras out to take pictures and it was: "No, no, no – no pictures." We weren't allowed to – but we did sneak a few. We got about three or four thousand pounds in prize money. Their money was no good in England, so a few of us got together on a street corner and gave it away. People wouldn't take it for a start, because they thought it was a gag, you know, something to do with authority, and that they'd be in trouble. Anyhow, we got rid of it all eventually.'

There were also regular jaunts to continental Europe organized by Trevor Redmond. Ron says: 'In those days you could have made a living just racing. I could earn £80-85 a night, which was quite good pay really. Plus I had my expenses paid. I used to stipulate a signing-on fee of £1,000 – but that was peanuts compared with what they get paid now – it's millions today.

'In 1961 I decided to give up speedway and carry on with the business. I did miss racing. I didn't know what to do with myself for a while.'

There were health problems. He says: 'It hasn't been very good since I had my stomach removed in 2009. They thought they'd got all the cancer out but they hadn't, and we didn't know that until later. I had aorta troubles, so I had that fixed, and after that I had a blood clot, which they acted on very quickly because otherwise I would have lost my legs. The trouble is that the cancer spread into the bladder and bowel. I had an urgent operation for bowel cancer. So there's really no recovery from any of that now. I just have to live in hope.'

'Some advice: My father used to say, if you want something, save up for it instead of putting it on hire purchase. Also, if you want to do something, do it. Go about it in a positive way, and you'll succeed. I've always said that if I wanted to make something, I would, so I either made it or waited until I could buy it. Most of the time I could just make it, and think nothing of it.'

Ron was always independent minded. He sacrificed part of the 1956 season as a protest against new tyre regulations, but eventually got back on a bike and picked up where he had left off.

He represented his country in 16 internationals and though largely out-dazzled by the Craven magic at club level, under Ron's captaincy the Aces won the Britannia Shield three times and the Daily Mail National Trophy. He remains one of the best New Zealanders to have graced the sport and one of the Manchester side's finest.

Johnno's health problems finally caught up with him and he died aged eighty-four in 2014.

White liner ... Ron, in typical stand-up style, hugs the inside at Hyde Road.

Ron Clarke
ONLY THE BEST FOR THE JOKER

To look at him, you wouldn't guess the gent reclining in that rather unconventional situation with a rather smug smile on his face, looking for all the world part of an old-style music hall comedy routine about to be on the receiving end of a traditional slapstick custard pie, that in his day he was described as 'the best team skipper bar none in the First Division of the National League'.

Now would you? Well he is … or was.

Apart from supplying the somewhat vintage apurtenance in the wash-and-brush-up department, room service appears to have come up with a delivery of morning tea – in a china cup, no less, and a saucer.

Yes, in those days, world class international speedway stars certainly knew how to live the high life. The 'gent' in question was England and Bradford's Ron Clarke, described as 'the embodiment of speedway mischief fun and games – still the overgrown schoolboy', and a bit of a joker.

Ron was never one to take life too seriously as can be deduced by the condition of the hat he is wearing. It has that mistreated appearance typical of one of the numerous titfers formerly owned by promoting doyen Johnnie S. Hoskins which were continually abused by impetuous, fun-loving speedway riders such as Mr Clarke. For their own amusement … and the crowd's of course.

Living the high life … Ron Clarke, the joker, enjoying his particular brand of fun.

Today Ron's daughter Diana says: 'It's true. My Dad was a joker. And very funny. He had a lively personality. At one of the speedway events my mother said: "Look at that." Everyone was around him. He was very popular.'

There is a 30-line account of Ron Clarke's racing career in a booklet entitled *Who's Who In Speedway* dated 1949 … but it's as dry as dust.

The actual real, living, breathing Ron Clarke is revealed in another publication, *Speedway Favourites,* dated two years earlier. I cannot do better than quote from it because, to my mind, it is an insight into the essential character of the man.

Under the daunting heading Harringay Did Not Want Ron, you get this: 'Tall, keen-looking Ron Clarke, with the air of a daredevil and just a hint of the swashbuckling buccaneer, was one of the shock riders of the 1946 season … '

There, in the space of a single sentence, is the essence of his personality.

Diana says: 'There is a picture of him in a ballet dress. Him and Oliver Hart … the majorettes, marching girls who used to put on displays at meetings, he had one of their dresses on and the pair of them were raking the cinders.'

Even weeding the garden was done in an unconventional way. Diana says: My Dad weeded the garden with a blowtorch. He was out in the garden burning up everything. No one else would do that. He was sort of crazy.'

One biography has Ron being born in Oxford and another in Cambridge. So he had the best high flying correct credentials from the start. But they both agree that the year of his birth was 1914.

He began racing on the Sunday junior tracks and that famous speedway academy Rye House. Diana says: 'My mother had a big family and he would take her and her sisters to Rye House. When he drove into the stadium they would say: "Here comes Clarkie with his harem."' They got married in 1936, just after he started at Rye House.

Making his way in the speedway world at Lea Bridge before the war with some of his fellow aspiring young stars … and one old timer who was no doubt teaching them the finer points of the game: That was Gus Kuhn, formerly of Stamford Bridge, Wembley, Wimbledon, Southampton and Lea Bridge … which was how he came to be instructing the young hopefuls there. He is on the extreme left and Ron Clarke is right next to him. Also in the line-up is Dick Harris (Wimbledon), fourth from left, and next to him Will Lowther (Glasgow).

Making progress against the big names in a wartime meeting at Belle Vue, leading Norman Parker and Oliver Hart.

Daughter Diana with her Dad indulging in one of their favourite pleasures … reading comics.

'He wanted to progress, so when he was offered the chance to go to Australia he took it. He had to pay for himself, though maybe his father, who had a haulage business, helped him to go. It was only six months after they were married so my mother was left behind. She had a shop so she couldn't really go. It probably didn't bother her too much – she knew speedway was going to be his profession.'

When he returned from Australia, Ron landed a Harringay contract by winning a match race against future Belle Vue and Wimbledon star Ron Mason. But because of his lack of experience he didn't get a place in what was a star-studded league side. There was the occasional appearance at Crystal Palace on Saturday afternoons in 1939 but nothing to indicate he was a potential world-beater.

Then came the war years and the regular 'We Never Closed' Belle Vue, Hitler-defying Saturday meetings that kept the sport alive during hostilities. In the stellar company of such world class international big names as Frank Varey, Bill Kitchen, Eric and Oliver Langton, Jack and Norman Parker, Ron Johnson, Tommy Price, Morian Hansen, Alec Statham and Eric Chitty, Ron Clarke began to blossom. And so did his pal Oliver Hart.

Chitty, another early pre-war struggler who had been on the verge of being sacked by his West Ham boss, the fiery Hoskins, emerged to monopolise the wartime British Championships by winning three successive titles between 1940 and 1942, until Ron Clarke put a stop to his gallop in 1943. They linked up the following year and the partnership won the British Empire Best Pairs.

He had arrived. And Hoskins, who knew a thing or two about speedway talent, chose Ron alongside Alec Statham and Ernie Price from the team equalising rider pool for his new enterprise, the Boomerangs, at Bradford in 1946.

Hoskins, it was suggested, picked riders 'with the abandonment of one who was convinced that the whole world was against him anyway so it didn't matter a lot which riders he selected'. But Johnnie's team of unfashionables was the cause of much envy from other clubs before the season was very old – a great deal of it down to Ron Clarke who not only outscored his Odsal team mates, but also top liners Ron Johnson of New Cross, Eric Langton of Belle Vue and Norman Parker of Wimbledon.

And then, as he was on the brink of real stardom, a just reward for the

Super captain – 'one of the best in the game': Ron was an old-style team rider and he is 'educating' the then young and inexperienced Jack Biggs.

NEW SPEEDWAY MOTOR CYCLE FRAME

RON CLARK, well-known Bradford rider, is seen in the accompanying illustration leaning on the motor cycle frame which he and "Friar" Tuck, also of Bradford, have designed, and which is now being manufactured by O.E.C., who are producing at the rate of eight frames a week.

This is the first all-welded frame to be produced, and it is in three units, the front fork, the centre frame section, and the rear section, which are bolted together.

One decided attraction about this frame, from the point of view of the ordinary motor cyclist, is the cost, which is comparatively low.

Novel Feature

The novel feature of the frame is that it can take any make of engine, wheels and handlebars, and seems to be ideally suitable for novices on grass and dirt tracks. The frame itself, once assembled, is very stout, and can stand up to a good deal of rough handling.

Publicity for the revolutionary low cost, robust speedway frame designed and marketed by Ron and team mate Fred Tuck.

Above left: *The inseprables: Close friends on the track … and business partners off it. Oliver Hart and Ron in earnest discussion. Note the extra pad on Oliver's knee – to protect it because his leg-trailing style meant his knee was in constant contact with the track surface.*

Above right: *The team of unfashionables. Ron leads the smiling Odsal side of 1949 – 'the happiest bunch in the business': From left Oliver Hart, Ernie Price, Norman Price, Ron, Jack Biggs, Bob Lovell, Joe Abbott and Eddie Rigg. Behind, Bruce Booth, who succeeded Johnnie Hoskins as promoter, and manager Eric Langton.*

Right: *In command: The highly accomplished style that gave the opposition headaches, Ron at Harringay, the club that rejected him before the war.*

Above left: *Chums … Ron and feathered friend, a jackdaw, called – amazingly enough – Jackie. Daughter Diana said: 'The jackdaw belonged to my aunt and uncle who lived next door to us. It kept flying into our house.' The relationship resulted in a special feature in the speedway press, and joker Ron told the reporter: 'He's a grand little fellow, he smokes cigarettes, lifts the lid off the teapot and does everything but ride for the Boomerangs.'*

Above right: *Serious business … sometimes: Ron takes a quiet moment to get himself psyched up for action. But he had a rather prominent nose, and after one hectic tussle with George Wilks at West Ham he just scraped past the flag first. As they came into the pits Ron cracked: 'Good race George. I must have won by a nose.'*

Just one of those things: Ron carries out his captain's duties even while recovering from another fractured leg and discusses tactics with Lloyd Goffe, then riding for Bradford.

work and sacrifices of more than a decade, it all came crashing down. Literally.

He was a 'surprise' choice for the England side in the first post-war Test – though his scintillating form would suggest he should have been no surprise at all, especially as it took place on his home track at Odsal. He partnered his Bradford skipper Alec Statham to three heat wins in the 65 – 43 victory over Australia and then, in his final ride, he crashed trying to go round Australia's Frank Dolan on the last bend of the last race of the evening and was carried off with a broken leg. The injury meant he was out of action for a large part of the season.

Ron spent a decade at Bradford, succeeding as captain when Alec Statham left for Wimbledon, and establishing a fine reputation as one of the best captains in the game. His popularity grew – among fans home and away, and among his team mates.

Ron was a team rider of the old school, and to be paired with Clarkie was considered a privilege and an education. The members of his team were said to be the happiest bunch of boys in the business. Any of the Odsal youngsters who rode with Ron would have told you that with him behind you all you had to do was keep going as Clarkie gave the opposition a headache.

His daughter Diana recalls: 'At his funeral people said: "You know your Dad would stay back to let the younger riders go first and he let them win." He was always willing to give up points for younger riders such as Arthur Forrest, Arthur Wright and Nigel Boocock – he was lovely.

'I don't think he was tremendously ambitious. I think he loved it, but never said to me he wanted to be a champion. He just liked racing and he was very supportive of the boys he rode with.'

At the time, speedway riders were like modern pop stars and crowds were enormous.

Not happy at all, looking decidedly uncomfortable wearing the 'alien' Lancastrian Belle Vue race jacket in 1957 after so long with Bradford and the Yorkshire club had closed down.

'They were all very famous,' Diana says. 'When the local children saw the bikes outside they would come to the house for autographs. As a child I didn't understand it. He would take me to Bradford and we would be walking into the stadium and the people would all come running around. I never thought: my Dad's famous. He was just my Dad.

'We lived at Harlesden, in northwest London, and when Dad was racing at Wembley we would leave our house and the roads were chock-a-block, you couldn't get there. Once we had a police escort to reach the stadium. I have very fond memories of the speedway. I was born in 1943, the only baby. My earliest recollection is when I was five and we went to Australia.

'My mother didn't like the danger part. She would go to the meetings but when it was his race she would hide her face. He did sometimes come home bruised and battered.'

Diana was friends with the children of Wembley captain Bill Kitchen and the children of Aub Lawson of West Ham. How did they all get on?

'We never argued among ourselves,' she says. 'When we went to the tracks we would all be cheering for our own Dads. It was a vey social sort of life. Dad was friends even with the opposition. I see that these days footballers don't like the other team. Well that never happened in speedway. It was all very congenial. Dad would never talk about his opponents. There was only one he didn't like too much because he felt he wasn't a clean rider, but I can't think who he was.'

One of Ron's more colourful team mates was Fred 'Friar' Tuck. The pair of them marketed the revolutionary EOC speedway frame. They were very good friends on and off the track, but the relationship was not always sweetness and light.

Diana remembers: 'Fred sold us a car. It was an old car but it had tables that came down in the back. My Dad said it was the worst car he ever had. He once said: "I'll kill that Fred."

Veterans gathering. Long after casting off their leathers Ron, right, gets together with two old speedway opponents and friends, Jack Gordon, centre, and Phil 'Tiger' Hart.

'He was very superstitious. Anything to do with 13, and he wouidn't walk under a ladder. Friday was an absolute no-no. If the 13th happened to be on a Friday he wouldn't race. I came home on a Thursday the 12th and he phoned me the next day and said: "Don't go out in the car today." I said: "You are the one who is superstitious, not me.

'He was huge friends with Oliver Hart. They were inseperable. And they went into business together.' When they weren't racing on the speedways they were both successful haulage contractors.

Ron raced until the age of forty-six. In a career spanning twenty-four years he qualified for two consecutive World Finals, in 1949 and 1950, and there were nine appearances for England. But after recovering from another broken leg at Harringay in 1951 he struggled and he decided he'd had enough in 1957 when Bradford closed down.

After a brief and uncomfortable looking appearance for Belle Vue he was persuaded to make a comeback with Sheffield in 1960 in the then thriving Provincial League which tempted many veterans like Ron to return. But he rode in only one match before quitting for good.

Diana says: 'He and Oliver promoted at Odsal for a while, and then there was a problem, apparently with the speedway authorities, so they just gave up. But he would still go to the speedway. He took me to Leicester one day and I thought it was not like it used to be. Like now, it doesn't interest me now.

'People of my generation remember how wonderful it all was. It's not the same any more … and the smell (of burned castor oil and methanol). Didn't we love that smell?

'I got a speeding ticket the other day. I thought only my Dad got those. My Dad was stopped three times in one day, I think on his way to Bradford. He was a speed demon.

'I put up a plaque to my Dad in the Speedway Museum memorial garden at the Paradise Wildlife Park, and they left the 'e' off his name.

'But it was lovely. I did like that.'

On display, the Clarke memorabilia. Some years after Ron's death daughter Diana donated Ron's Odsal blazer to the National Speedway Museum at Broxbourne, Hertfordshire, and the author (far right) was deputed – and honoured - to wear it at the handing over ceremony. Present were former Wembley captain Bert Harkins, left, World Speedway Riders Association Secretary Peter Sampson, curator of the museum, and double World Champion Fred Williams, appropriately on the bike.

Eric Chitty

DAMES . . . AND THE SPEEDWAY TROUBADOR

T HE ACT WAS ONE of utter selflessness, and a sporting gesture that was to earn the accolade 'speedway's greatest racing brain'. And it was part of a technique that was to merit the gratitude of many a wannabe track star of the future.

Yet, as with any sporting personality with a world class reputation to maintain, whose chosen profession compels him to live on the edge, an abrasive ruthlessness tended to lurk just below the surface charm.

To discover who this paragon is we must first go back a little over three-quarters of a century to a memorable night in 1938. It was Wednesday May 18, the night that wonderful little stadium at New Cross just off the Old Kent Road in south London staged the seventh London Riders Championship.

The line-up had the strength of a traditional one-off World Final. The finest speedway riders on earth were on parade that night, including reigning World Champion Jack Milne, riding on his home track, former World Champion Lionel Van Praag of Wembley, the in-form contenders for that year's title Wilbur Lamoreaux of Wimbledon, Bluey Wilkinson and Arthur Atkinson of West Ham plus Jack Parker of Harringay.

Along with track specialist Stan Greatrex, there was also West Ham's Eric Chitty, who was in only his third season of racing with the big boys in Britain. And little more than 18 months earlier, because of his poor performances, he had been in danger of being sacked by his irascible firebrand promoter of a boss, the self-styled Admiral of Barking Creek, Johnnie S. Hoskins.

There were 16 qualifying heats and, against all that was reasonable, Eric Chitty made it to the final along with holder Jack Milne and Van Praag. On a saturated track Milne and Van Praag got in each other's way on the first turn and the unfashionable Eric picked his way delicately through the mayhem to take the title.

On the way, and this was a measure of the man, as Van Praag remounted following his tangle with Milne, instead of lapping the Wembley captain and so putting him out of the race, Chitty knocked off his throttle to enable Van Praag to finish and take second place … and the £10 in prize money.

The leading speedway magazine of the day, *Speedway News*, reported that 'however finely though he rode, Eric would be the first to admit he was largely indebted to fortune for his biggest honour so far … '

Well … maybe. But I'm not so sure about that.

I find myself at odds with the *Speedway News* assessment of the Chitty victory that damp night at New Cross. Kipling's immortal words from his poem *If* spring to mind: *'If you can keep your head when all about you are losing theirs …'* They seem to fit the occasion somehow.

The special attraction. An early poster for a Grand Dance advertising Eric in his other role as the Crooning Speedway Star.

Glamour shot. For fan consumption, a publicity picture as befits the image of a troubador.

One of Johnnie's jaunts that went wrong: Hoskins was renowned for his exotic crowd-pulling interval attractions but he was caught out on this particular piece of hooey, a bike v cheetah contest. The Admiral of Barking Creek was exposed as the biggest 'cheater' of the night and Eric had to tether his furry friend in case it escaped.

But, let's see. Hands up all those who have been present when a flag bearing the single heraldic symbol of a scarlet maple leaf has been hoisted at a speedway meeting while *O Canada,* the senior dominion's national anthem, has blared forth from the public address system and everyone has risen to hats-off attention in honour of the rider standing on the rostrum with No.1 painted on it.

… Yes, as I thought … precious few.

Unless, of course, you had happened to be at New Cross that particular night in 1938. It was almost certainly the one and only time in speedway history that the Canadian flag was unfurled to signify that a Canuck had walked off with the major prize. I invite any smart-Alec historian who can prove otherwise to write in.

Were he around today, Eric Stephenson Chitty would very possibly have considered it true that the moment was his – and Canada's – most meritorious speedway hour. But, as we shall see, the best of Eric Chitty was really still to come.

Eric Chitty, born Toronto 1909, has been described as the most successful Canadian speedway rider to visit Britain. It was a statement made by the astute and knowledgable speedway journalist Tom *Broadsider* Morgan in his booklet *Who's Who In Speedway* of 1949.

Pre-war enthusiasts, particularly Brough Park regulars, will want to remind us of the brilliant George Pepper, who just might have topped Chitty had he not been killed in a wartime flying accident.

Others will want to mention Goldie Restall of New Cross, and of course the likes of Bill Maddern, Bruce Venier, Elwood Stilwell, Charlie Appleby and the only man who ran Chitty anything like close, Jimmy Gibb of West Ham and Wimbledon who, at the last count, was still going strong having passed his 102nd birthday, but sadly is now riding the great celestial cinder circuit.

Modern fans may mention Shawn Venables, briefly of Hackney and Belle Vue, and then there was Krzysztof Slabon – who rode under a flag of convenience, a Canadian licence, but was actually Polish.

Eric, in prominent maple leaf helmet, and Eugenie, who started out as his sidecar passenger and appears to have been demoted to humble pusher-off, at the Custom House Stadium, West Ham, giving a ride to daughter Carol … who looks rather less than thrilled.

Eric Chitty qualified for the 1938 and 1939 World Finals plus the three substitute World Finals at Wembley in 1946, 1947 and 1948. Jimmy Gibb (motto 'Never Gibb Up') made the 1938 World Final as a reserve. And though the pair of them boosted pre-war Canadian and Overseas sides in Britain, the others where not really in the same class.

So Chitty had a lot going for him, after his near disastrous British debut, that is, which may be the reason his name usually appears as an also-ran when speedway aficionados set about assessing the world's best: he *was* rated number ten in the World Rankings three years running from 1947.

Actually he was in no real hurry to try his luck on the cinder tracks of Britain. In Toronto he had shown himself to be determined and un-orthodox. As a young apprentice electrical engineer he was once sworn at by his boss, so he walked out and refused to go back. No amount of uproar over the walkout would change his mind. His father had been a lay preacher so he had a fairly strict upbringing.

Getting down to a discussion in the famous West Ham silver sand surface, Eric with team mate Phil Bishop. There is a marked contrast in the depth of the pre-war track surface compared to that of present day tracks.

In his contribution to the Stenner's *My Story* series just after the war he revealed that he had met a Miss Eugenie Stead at a motorcycle scramble event and persuaded her to be his sidecar passenger in club competitions. He wrote: 'To have a dame as a passenger … well … some of the other competitors nearly exploded. But we took first place at 75 mph – and we've been together ever since. In due course she became my wife.' There was, many years later, a divorce.

Within a few years speedway mania had hit North America, as it had in Australia and Britain, and the motorcycle mad Chitty was in on it, riding at Chicago, Indiana, Milwaukee and Detroit as well as Toronto. The only trouble was, all the travelling and the medical bills from his frequent crashes swallowed up nearly all his winnings.

Johnnie Hoskins, on one of his many excursions between England and Australia via America, spotted Eric's potential. But the newly married Chitty considered the offer of a West Ham contract for a year before doing anything about it.

He was broke again, so he cabled Hoskins and by return received the one-way fare to England. His father found the cash to pay for Eugenie and their daughter Carol. When they arrived at Victoria station in London the Chittys had a ten shilling (50p) note to their name.

Hoskins's West Ham partner, Victor Martin, of Martin-JAP speedway machine fame, gave Eric an advance of £100 to tide them over. Eric wrote: 'My next worry was; could I live up to my publicity reputation?' In true Hoskins hyperbole, the Old Warhorse had told all London he had signed the Canadian champion for his Hammers. And Eric was about to discover just how tough English speedway, 1936 style, could be.

'For two meetings I couldn't do a thing,' he confessed. 'On the third night I fell off in front of an opponent. He couldn't avoid me and the collision resulted in a broken kneecap.

'I couldn't afford to lay off racing for even a short while. That £100 had dwindled steadily, so I rode with the knee the size of a balloon. I cut down on meals and spent a lot of time in bed resting the knee. I felt I couldn't let on to the management I was in such a state, they had already been so good to me.'

Hoskins's Hammers of 1936, the side that finished stone last in the league, and the following year went on to win the First Division title. From left: Johnnie Hoskins, Eric, Arthur Atkinson, Bluey Wilkinson, Ken Brett, Mick Murphy, Tommy Croombs, Rol Stobart, Stan Dell, Phil Bishop and Harold 'Tiger' Stevenson.

Proudly parading the silverwear, Hoskins's Hammers of 1938. Riders from left: Harry Saunders, Ted Vigor, Phil Bishop, Dick Geary, Hoskins, Aussie Powell, Ed Barker, Jimmy Gibb. Sitting: Eric, Arthur Atkinson, Bluey Wilkinson the 1938 World Champion behind the tall World Championship trophy, Harold 'Tiger' Stevenson and Tommy Croombs.

Things were about as bad as they could be. Johnnie's Hammers were bottom of the league and he was ready to sack his Canadian 'discovery'. If it hadn't been for the intervention of *Broadsider* Morgan of *The People* newspaper he would have done. It was the same *Broadsider* Morgan who was to write such a glowing endorsement of Eric in his little booklet thirteen years later.

Morgan recalled: 'Eric's difficulties centred around new bikes, new tracks, a new country and in the background an impatient Hoskins who had expected his new "champion" to tear down the roof as soon as he stepped off the boat.

'I had seen Eric ride and guessed he wasn't half as bad as he looked. I said so in print and in public. And when I got the ear of Hoskins the old so-and-so was in a more benevolent mood.'

Hoskins agreed to 'give the kid another chance'.

Eric said: 'I was recalled to the Hammers and from then on Dame Fortune – whose acqaintance I had never known on the cinders – smiled on me. Though that Dame still had a few hard knocks in store for me.'

And as the fortunes of Eric Chitty began to take an upswing, so did those of Hoskins's Unhappy Hammers. The same side that won the wooden spoon in 1936 zoomed to the top of the league a year later. Hoskins attributed the phenomenal change to 'a heart full of hope and a hatful of hooey.'

Part of the hooey involved Eric Chitty. Hoskins, famed for his unconventional interval attractions, laid on the most incredible crowd-drawing match race in the history of speedway – Eric and his speedway bike versus a real live cheetah.

But just before the tapes were due to rise on the amazing event it was discovered that crowd safety decreed it was not permitted for a live, flesh-eating predator with such a ferocious reputation to be let loose in a stadium containing something like 40,000 live, and potentially succulent, human beings.

So Roarin' John had to settle for some newsworthy pictures of Eric with the tethered beastie and an invitation to the general speedway public to guess who at West Ham was the night's biggest 'cheater'.

Fortunately for the Hoskins publicity machine, Eric was also a crooner of no mean ability. He not only sang to the Custom House crowd during meeting intervals, he made gramophone records too. And long before Sinatra had the bobby-soxers swooning, the Chitty effect had girl fans rushing the stage, even fainting away, whenever he took to the mic at supporters club dances, when he became known as the Troubador Of The Speedways.

Dark days at wartime Belle Vue, where Eric was outstanding. This powerful side, all regulars at the makeshift meetings, is, from the left: Wilf Plant, Bill Longley, Eric on the bike, Bill Pitcher, Tommy Price, Jack Parker and Wally Lloyd.

If anyone in speedway had any doubts whatsoever that Eric Chitty had arrived in the big time, even after his London Riders Championship win, the war years would have dispelled them. Eric contributed to the war effort in an aircraft factory and continued to ride in the Saturday afternoon meetings at Belle Vue throughout the conflict.

It was at Hyde Road that Eric became the first rider to win the triple crown, three 'world championships' in succession, pre-empting Ivan Mauger's in 1968, 1969 and 1970 by nearly thirty years.

Okay … so they weren't the official World Championships, they were the wartime British Individual Championships staged at Manchester when the likes of the Parker brothers, Ron Johnson, Tommy Price, Frank Varey, Eric Langton and Bill Kitchen – all at the time world class – were also regulars. Eric won the title in 1940, 1941 and 1942.

Real progress, Eric is elevated to the captaincy of West Ham in 1946. Behind him are Benny King, Bob Harrison, Buck Whitby, Cyril Anderson, Malcolm Craven, Ron Howes and Jack Cooley.

He also won the Northern Championship, the Speedway Derby, the Hundred Guineas Trophy, The National trophy, the All-England Best Pairs with Fred Tuck and the British Empire Best Pairs with Ron Clarke.

When full-time league racing resumed in the war weary days of the late 1940s speedway enjoyed fabulous popularity with the British sporting public, the likes of which it had never previously known. Can you imagine a full house at the great Wembley arena every week for a mere speedway league match? In those days it happened.

With the pre-war West Ham superstars gone: Bluey Wilkinson, killed ironically in a motorcycle road accident in Australia, and Tiger Stevenson and Arthur Atkinson retired, Eric found himself captain of the Hammers. He was an inspiration. His skill as a team man and a tactician became legendary.

He had matured into a great captain, even leading the most unusual speedway team ever assembled in the sport's history, the all-star ENSA side that toured Europe in the winter of 1945-46 to entertain the Allied occupying forces. Another tour was planned the following winter but that turned into a disaster. Not Eric's fault, the Continental promoters pulled out at the last minute.

The unique racing style of Eric Chitty who, even when wide cowhorn handlebars became fashionable, always preferred to ride with his straight and narrow.

Passing on the knowledge ... pre-war Hammers ace Arthur Atkinson, left, gave up promoting at West Ham not long after the war to make a brief return to the track, and though a veteran with much more experience than Eric, he appears to be listening intently to the Chitty advice.

The high point at this time for him was his fourth place in the 1947 Speedway Riders Championship behind Belle Vue's Jack Parker, Wembley's Bill Kitchen and New Cross's Bill Longley.

Then it seemed that the Dame he had referred to long ago – the one with 'a few hard knocks still in store for me' – remembered and was waiting for him.

After the 1947 Continental debacle, he joined the revived close season exodus to Australia and during the 1948-49 tour he crashed and broke a leg at Brisbane only hours before he was due to sail for the new season in Britain. He recovered eventually and rode again, but he was never quite the force he had been. When he broke a leg again in a fall from a horse it was the end of his track career.

And that force extended to his personality, on and off the track. He had been secretary of the strong riders union, the Speedway Riders Association (SRA), and the youthful up-and-coming Wally Green recalled an incident involving 'the other side' of Eric Chitty soon after being recalled to West Ham from Third Division Hastings.

Wally said: 'I was called back to be a reserve in an open meeting. In Heat 4 I had to go out with Chitty, and as I was a phenomenally fast starter I got out first and came out of the first turn in front. Chitty came alongside me on the outside and then turned left on me, cutting onto the inside halfway down the straight. I came off and broke my collarbone.
'A couple of weeks later, still strapped up, I went along to West Ham to watch a meeting. Chitty kept walking past me all night in the pits – completely ignoring me. Towards the end of the meeting, he came up to me and stared me straight in the face and said to me: "I tell you something: don't ever try and beat me round West Ham." And he wagged his finger at me as if to say: I taught you a lesson.

'The sequel to that came years later in some cup competition at Edinburgh. Of course the king of Edinburgh was Jack Young. I won my first race and in my second race I had Eric Chitty with me as my partner – he was reserve then – against Jack Young. I was concentrating on trying to beat Jack Young, which was almost impossible because virtually nobody beat Jack Young round Edinburgh.

The only fellow Canadian to be in the same class as Eric Chitty, Jimmy Gibb, here with Alec Statham in Wimbledon colours.

'Chitty came up to me and said: "Will you help me round the first corner?" I more or less agreed that I would – though I knew I wouldn't after what he did to me. The tapes went up and I shot out with Youngie behind me and we went down the back straight. Three quarters of the way round the next bend Youngie came past me like a dose of salts – he came past me so fast ... and just then the red lights came on.

'Chitty had fallen off. And he never raced again. I thought that perhaps if I'd helped him round the first corner maybe he wouldn't have been hurt. And then I thought: You can't say that Wally, he didn't consider you when he broke your collarbone, and he did it deliberately.'

Wally Green got nearer the world title than ever Eric did, he finished second to Fred Williams in 1950, just one point away from the major prize.

Eric rode only for the Hammers, and Tom Morgan once wrote of him: 'Eric is part of West Ham and it is inconceivable that he would ride for any other team. Only on the day that Eric Chitty leaves West Ham will I believe that there will be no more speedway racing at the Custom House stadium.'

In the end, of course, Eric did go. And so did the Custom House stadium. Johnnie Hoskins, in one of his wilder and more extravagant moments, attempted to perpetrate the myth that West Ham had a ghost. No one believed him.

And yet I wonder ... Eric Chitty died in 1990 at the age of eighty-one after returning to his native Canada. As the mists rise in these damp, dark days along the lower reaches of London's Dockland, and perhaps curl their clammy fingers around the enamel nameplates on Hoskins Close, Wilkinson Road, Atkinson Road and Young Road, could it be that the locals now living on the site where the old West Ham stadium used to be might hear the spectral sound of a speedway motor being warmed up round about 7.45pm on Tuesday nights.

And I wonder too whether, if they cared to go in search of the source, they might catch a glimpse of a shadowy handsome phantom figure in shining leathers standing where the old racing pits used to be.

Ole Olsen
THE OTHER GOLD BIKE

YOU HAVE HEARD OF The Gold Bike. *THE* Gold Bike. The entire speedway world knows about it. The bike was gold plated for Ivan Mauger to mark him winning three consecutive World Championships in 1968, 1969 and 1970.

Well, there *IS* another Gold Bike. And not many people know that.

It belongs to the man who put a stop to the Mauger World Championship steamroller, Ole Olsen of Denmark, who won the first of his three world titles in 1971.

Ole says: 'The story is that it was the bike I won my first World Championship on in 1971. I kept that bike. It was up in my loft in Denmark. I'd had it there for years. Obviously you do not throw things like that out.

Dir. Tove Nørgaard, Hotel Norden og Ole Olsen fotograferet i Hotel Nordens reception ved Ole Olsens VM-cykel forgyldt af Robert Jacobsen.

Der sker noget på Hotel Norden.

Hotel Norden
Storegade 55 · 6100 Haderslev · Tlf. 04 52 40 30
Sveaborg Hotel & Conference Group

The words in the top right of the picture read:
'Hotel Norden is also in the top form to the World Championship in Speedway '88 and bid the speedway elite welcome!'

The words under Ole and the hotel manager read: 'Manager Tove Norgaard, Hotel Norden and Ole Olsen photographed in Hotel Norden's reception in front of Ole Olsen's World Championship bike gilt by Robert Jacobsen.'

The words under the golden helmet and rear wheel read: 'Things happen at Hotel Norden.'

'Suddenly there was a famous artist and sculptor in Denmark called Robert Jacobsen. He has followed speedway all the time – he saw me at Wembley and everywhere. There was a big hotel being renovated in Haderslev, the Hotel Norden, and they asked him to decorate it with his pictures and sculptures. He walked into the foyer with a lot of people behind him, you know how these artists are – he died in 1993 when he was 81 – and he said that he would put a picture here and a sculpture there. And in the foyer he said: "Here I want something local, and I want something international … I want Ole Olsen's bike!"

'Well, everyone is looking at him and wondering: Ole Olsen's bike? They couldn't believe it.

'Anyway, he puts all these things in and then he calls me and says: "Ole, I want your bike." And when I asked him why he said he was going to make a sculpture of it.

'But I said I wouldn't give it to him because I thought he was going to saw it in half and weld it together, like they do. I thought I'd have to think about what I should do, so I said: "Call me tomorrow." So he calls me and says:

World Champion: Ole Olsen on the Wembley podium in 1975 after winning his second World title.

The other *gold bike – Ivan Mauger's original, for winning the Triple Crown, three successive World Championships.*

"You will love it. It will be a memento to you."

'So I said, OK, he could have it. And he had it all gold plated.

'It's like Ivan's. All gold plated – 24ct gold.

'It's there in the foyer of the hotel in a glass module. It's been there all the time, with my gold helmet and my FIM medal from 1971. And the bike is still mine. If they don't want it at some time – because you know how hotels change – it's been there since 1983 and it's had three owners in that time, and they all want to keep the bike. But my family can have it if they don't want it any more.

'I don't know how much it's worth – but I know it cost a lot of money to have it done. It does have sentimental value, of course, and as scrap metal it's not much. But it's the history. I was born in the city, I played round there by the lakes as a child, the hotel was there in my time as a child, but it was a very old type hotel then until it was renovated.

'And of course it has done a lot for motor sport in Denmark. You know, I was the first World Champion, and it was done by Robert Jacobsen, the most famous Danish artist ...'

The artwork of Robert Jacobsen.

Translation by Henrik Andersen, who explains: 'Robert Jacobsen is one of our most, if not the most, well known sculptors in Denmark and internationally known too.'

Jack Young

LAID BACK JACK . . . THE MAN WHO HAD ALMOST EVERYTHING

THEY CALLED HIM Laid Back Jack because of his temperament. And the Armchair Champion because of his smooth riding style. He is thought to have been the nearest thing to the perfect speedway rider, possessing seven out of ten of the must-have virtues.

Those who saw Jack Young ride were privileged in the extreme. He rose to fame with Edinburgh, which is why the Monarchs are forever blessed by an association with one of the true monarchs of the sport. Down all the near ninety-year history of speedway in Edinburgh there has never been any other single rider to match Youngie, never mind surpass his achievements.

New arrival: Jack, second from right after his dream debut with the 1949 Edinburgh team. From the left they are: Dennis Parker, Dick Campbell, Don Cuppleditch, Danny Lee, Bill Baird. On the end Eddie Lack. Clem Mitchell, who made it happen for Jack, is on the machine.

A sensation from his first ride, he set a series of amazing scoring records, and in his third British season claimed a place in history which has never been equalled.

Young, from the unfashionable Second Division club north of the border, went to Wembley and outrode all the big international stars to be crowned World Champion. He was the first, and only, rider from the lower division to win the sport's supreme prize. A year later, he made yet more history by becoming the first to win two world titles in succession. He had by then joined the world class elite for a record transfer fee of £3,750, roughly equivalent to an astonishing £67,000 by today's values.

But all that was half way through the last century – in 1951 and 1952. To understand the impact of the Jack Young phenomenon, we have to go back to his beginnings.

Jack Ellis Young first rode speedway in 1947 at the Kilburn track in Adelaide. He was 22 at the time and today would be considered a late starter. His enormous natural talent did not become apparent until a local JAP importer provided him with decent machinery. It was when he started beating visiting internationals that word reached England about his potential.

A family man, Young at first hesitated about the initial approaches from British clubs. He doubted his own ability at that time. He said: 'I could have made the trip to England right after the war, but for one thing. I couldn't ride, and I knew it. I decided to hang fire until I knew I could ride. When I broke all Jack Biggs's records at Adelaide I figured I was good enough. Not before.'

Pre-war New Cross and Australian Test star Clem Mitchell, who had ridden for Edinburgh in 1948, eventually persuaded Young to join the club with a promise that if he didn't make the grade he would get him a job looking after Highland sheep to earn the money for his passage home. At the time former Belle Vue and England ace Frank Varey ran Edinburgh, which paid Young's fare over. Arriving in the Scottish capital at the start of the 1949 season on a one-way ticket with only a verbal offer – no written contract – he had no choice but to succeed.

Laid back Jack wearing his Monarch's race jacket.

His debut was the stuff of dreams. He lined up for the first time in the Monarchs' colours on 2 April against local rivals Ashfield and scored an immaculate 12 point maximum. Riders took a total of four rides then, league matches were over 14 heats and there were no tactical substitutes.

Quite obviously Edinburgh had signed a sensation, but the fans had to wait to see whether Young could satisfy their wildest expectations because, almost immediately, he was rushed to hospital with appendicitis. When he recovered it was as though he had never been away. From his first 18 starts he took 18 wins, and his form that season was such that he was called up as reserve to ride for Australia in the fifth and final Test at Bradford.

It was a salutary lesson. In the company of such major international names as England's Jack Parker, Dent Oliver and that year's World Champion Tommy Price, plus fellow Australians Aub Lawson and Graham Warren Jack Young could manage only one point.

Even so, he led the scorers in the second round of the World Championship alongside fellow Australian Bob Levernez, another Second Division rider making a big name for himself with Norwich, and Bristol's Fred Tuck. But his 10 points at Glasgow White City were not quite enough to get him into the Championship Round. Still, his league average for the year was 9.01.

He had a successful return home to Adelaide, and in 1950 his Edinburgh average crept up to 11.15. This time he did qualify for the World Final – his first of eight – finishing eighth on seven points. He admitted that the pace was a little too hot for him, but his natural talent was now being honed on such world class competition. It was obvious that the Monarchs had a huge star in their ranks. With Glasgow's Tommy Miller, and Ken LeBreton at Ashfield, Scottish speedway had never had it so good.

Young resisted the temptation to switch to a club in the First Division for one more year, and 1951 was even more sensational. In the ten-match early season North Shield series he recorded ten maximums, and in his home Division Two matches at Old Meadowbank he was also unbeaten. He rode in 29 league matches and scored a maximum in 25 of them. By now he was a major star in Test matches, helping Australia to a 4 – 1 series win over

Team mates at Edinburgh, Jack, left – already at home in Scotland with his tartan scarf – and behind him Don Cuppleditch, Harry Darling, centre, and Bob Mark.

England, and he was in constant demand for regular appearances on First Division tracks as an added attraction .

In the World Championship qualifiers he topped the second round with Tommy Miller on 30 points. Harringay's Jack Biggs led the Championship round on 29 points, which made him favourite for the title, while Young scraped in on 23 points – two above the drop zone – with Wimbledon's veteran Norman Parker and Ernie Roccio, Wembley's Eric Williams and Bob Leverenz.

The Wembley Final on Thursday, September 20 was destined to be packed with high drama, but Jack Young had a far from ideal build-up to the big night. Three days before the Final, on Monday, September 17, Monarchs were at home to Coventry. Young said: 'Clem Mitchell and I had

spent many long hours working on my bike for Wembley and I was eager for my first ride on it.

'I went out there on a good track, in perfect conditions, and came back after winning the first heat almost exhausted and thoroughly disgusted with the machine. I had been out there in one long slide from start to finish. It had been a terrible job keeping it in hand, and I knew that I wouldn't be able to do the trick on it at Wembley. In fact I despaired of winning any more races that night. What's more, I wasn¹t going to ride the machine again.'

Young's team mate Harold Fairhurst was watching, and said: 'Here, Jack, take mine. Give it a good try!'

'I did,' said Young. 'I felt like a World Champion on it. My old feeling of wellbeing returned and I had a long chat with Harold. The bike the big fellow had was originally built for me by Clem in our workshops. Harold readily gave me permission to use it in the Final and I spent half the night and most of Tuesday fixing in my own motor.

'That's the story of the bike which helped me win the title, and it underlines the completely unselfish camaraderie which was always a feature of Edinburgh speedway. While I owe Clem Mitchell so much for his technical brilliance, I cannot forget Harold, either.'

The 1951 World Championship Final is often described as the one Jack Biggs lost rather than the one Jack Young won. Biggs won his first four rides and, needing a single point from his final outing to become World Champion, he finished last in his fifth ride. It set up a monumentally dramatic climax to the meeting – a three-man run-off for the title between Biggs, England's Split Waterman and Young.

Above left: *Special match race at the County Ground: Jack ready to take on hard man Cyril Roger at Exeter.*

Above right: *The devoted family man: Jack at home with wife Joan, daughters Carol Anne and Paula and son Mark.*

Feet up: the 'armchair' approach of Jack Young at speed after his record transfer to West Ham.

Young had dropped points in his opening ride, to Biggs in his second and to Wimbledon's Ronnie Moore in his last. It had looked all over bar the formalities when the riders came out for the decisive Heat 19: reigning World Champion Fred Williams, West Ham's Aub Lawson, neither of whom could win the meeting, and Harringay's Split Waterman who needed the win to put him level with Young.

There have been many reports and theories about why and how Jack Biggs failed to score the single point he needed for the World crown. With a capacity 93,000 hyped-up crowd, there was certainly incredible pressure.

It is not unusual, when riders are so close to winning a meeting – especially a World Final – for them to find a way of asking opponents for a 'favour'. There was a phrase for trading points. It was 'can you cover for me?' It meant will you talk to the other riders and more or less ask them to stay out of my way?'

What happened prior to, and during, the crucial Heat 19 of the 1951 World Final has been discussed and dissected endlessly over the years, and what actually happened was dealt with in detail in our previous book, *Speedway Superheroes*.

In any event, Jack Biggs asked for no favours so, in the words of Fred Williams: 'We just went out and fixed him – we all moved out on the first turn. It's terrible really, but that's what we did, because he had said nothing.'

There had been an earlier torrid encounter between Young and Fred Williams in Heat 11, but how Young reacted to the incident says much about his temperament. With only four points in three rides, Williams's world crown was slipping away. He had finished last in the previous race.

Fred remembered: 'Young was really motoring. I made the gate but I could hear Youngie trying to come under me, and when that failed he tried to go round me. It must have been marvellous to watch. I was coming down the finishing straight on the third lap and he was right behind me. I left it late going into the turn and threw the back wheel out. It hit Youngie and I could hear the clanging and banging.

'Isn't it amazing how nasty you can be? I don't think I'm a nasty person, but I was thinking: well, that's Youngie through the bloody fence. But because we had got into a bit of a skirmish I was a little wide coming out of the turn – and Youngie came up on the inside. He put up with all that and then passed me on the inside. Back in the pits he came up to me and just said: "You bastard, Willy …" I really did think I had put him in trouble on that corner.'

Waterman won Heat 19 putting him on 12 points. Biggs, though finishing last, was also on 12 with another chance of the title. And Young's 12 put the Second Division sensation of the night back in as well. It was a cataclysmic moment for riders and spectators. The first triple run-off in the history of the competition and a severe test of the nerve of all three competitors.

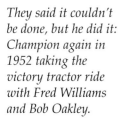

They said it couldn't be done, but he did it: Champion again in 1952 taking the victory tractor ride with Fred Williams and Bob Oakley.

Reigning champion: Jack at the head of the grand parade before the 1953 World Final at Wembley. To his left Dick Bradley, and behind Jack Biggs, Arthur Forrest, Olle Nygren and Ronnie Moore.

It was certainly a very poignant moment for Young because it had been when he had consistently beaten Jack Biggs's records at Adelaide as an unsure beginner that convinced him he might make it in Britain. And here he was lining up at Wembley against the master … for the world title … the sport's major prize.

But Young, who had been known as Mr Cool ever since his early days at Edinburgh, was unfazed. He said later that the two inside gate positions were unfavourable, and he had been on the inside when he met Biggs in the heats but had lost by only half a length. So he was full of confidence for the run-off.

Hammers clean up: Howdy Byford, Jack and Wally Green take the plunge after a meeting.

The number four gate position, which had produced 11 winners over the 20 heats, was ignored and in the draw Waterman was on one, Biggs on two and Young on three. Biggs, whose starting had been brilliant all night, except in Heat 19, led from the tapes, but Young was right with him and soon forced his way through. It took Waterman some time to eventually get past Biggs into second place but he could not catch the flying Young.

And so, the man from the Second Division confounded all the experts and became World Champion. He is reported to have commented after his victory: 'Gee – I'm that excited I could jump over the moon.' Maybe the world of football stole that now well-worn cliche from Jack Young.

His transfer to First Division West Ham in 1952, for a record £3,750 fee (almost £67,000 in today's values), produced 19 maximums from 38 league matches, followed by what the speedway world thought impossible, a successive second World Title, leaving no doubt that 1951 was no fluke and that he was the best and most consistent rider in the world at that time.

There were other titles, the London Riders Championship, the Golden Helmet British Match Race Championship but, just as he had ousted some of the old original veterans, even younger aspiring stars were ready to take over his mantle – Ronnie Moore, Barry Briggs, Peter Craven and Ove Fundin.

Yet as far as Young was concerned, speedway was not his sole reason for living. He was a family man who liked to enjoy life's simple pleasures. After his second World Final win he was severely criticised because he ignored pleas from West Ham supporters to be allowed to greet him as a conquering hero, going home to his wife and children in Adelaide five days after the World Final. He appeared only once for his club, at Coventry, scoring five points.

Speedway News magazine commented: 'No London track saw the Champion once he had secured the title. Playing the game? You, Mr and Mrs Cash customer, keep the game alive. Without you, fellows like Young couldn't earn the huge sums they do.'

Those 'huge sums' would certainly have been disputed by Young. His success never made him a rich man.

He never won an Australian National Championship because he preferred to go fishing rather than spend days travelling across the continent to compete. Though he did do some travelling through Australia with the emerging Ivan Mauger who credits Young with passing on invaluable advice and experience which aided his illustrious later career. After

The incident that effectively ended the career of veteran England and Wimbledon captain Norman Parker in the first Test of 1952. Closed down by Jack on the first turn, Parker is about to high side and crash, fracturing his skull.

Young retired it was typical of the man that he was reported to have used his World Championship trophy as a storage jar for his fishing weights!

When West Ham closed at the end of the 1955 season Young returned to Australia for a couple of years, then signed for Coventry. He remained a class act, and during his last season in England, 1961, he was able to work the old magic one last time when he won the Tom Farndon Trophy at New Cross, beating a field of top internationals that included Moore, Briggs, Craven and future World Champion Bjorn Knutsson. There were two more years racing in Australia before retirement in December 1963 after winning the South Australia State Championship.

Young died of a lung disorder on 28 August, 1987 aged sixty-two. He is still revered by older fans in Edinburgh and he has a street named after him on the housing site that used to be West Ham's Custom House stadium in London's Docklands.

His Old Meadowbank mentor Clem Mitchell is quoted as considering Young to have been the nearest thing to the perfect speedway rider. He said: 'In my opinion the perfect speedway rider must possess ten virtues. Jack has seven: an uncanny sense of balance; tenacity; the ability to see and seize opportunities; coolness at the gate; adaptability; a fearless and nerveless outlook; and an intense love of speedway.

The Australian international side at Wembley for the second Test against England in 1953. The Australians were one up in the three match series, but England won this one. From the left: Aub Lawson, Keith Gurtner, Arthur Simcock, manager, Jack, Ronnie Moore and Graham Warren. At the front Arthur Payne, Jack Biggs and Peter Moore.

'Maybe I'm biased in favour of Jack, who I knew as a lad in his home town of Adelaide, but there's no denying that he has nearly everything.'

Yes, it was a rare privilege to have witnessed the artistry of Mr Cool.

Additional material courtesy of Edinburgh Monarchs Official Website, Ross Garrigan, Mike Hunter, Neil Burston, Ian Hoskins and Classic Speedway Magazine.

Cool and unfazed: the immaculate Mr Young, wearing the Australian kangaroo, strikes a nonchalant pose in the Belle Vue pits before a Test match in 1950.

Below left: After the demise of West Ham, Jack reappeared briefly for Coventry in the 1960s. From the left, Nigel Boocock, Les Owen, Jim Lightfoot, Ron Mountford, Nick Nicholls, Kas Bentre and Bob Mark, manager. Jack is on the bike.

Below right: He's a visiting opponent, but Jack is consulted by home riders Louis Lawson and Bob Fletcher of Belle Vue to help solve a bike problem.

Fred Williams

THE JEKYLL AND HYDE WORLD CHAMPION

L ONG BEFORE TEAM ENGLAND'S most shining hour, the Grand Slam year of 1980 when Britannia really did rule the speedway waves by winning the World Team Cup, Pairs and Individual titles, Britain could rejoice in four World Champions in five years: Tommy Price in 1949, Fred Williams in 1950 and 1953, and Peter Craven in 1955.

England swept the board in 1949 with Jack Parker and Louis Lawson mounting the Wembley rostrum with Price. For the next five years British riders claimed second place, and one a third place. There were another two third places in 1956 and 1957.

That's 14 rostrum places in eight years. A proud record.

Of course Peter Craven won again in 1962, but that was it for fourteen years until Peter Collins in 1976.

We are concerned here with the only other British rider to win two world titles. Yes, besides The Wizard Of Balance, Fred Williams did it. Fred was Welsh, but British nonetheless.

And it is an iniquitous injustice that his name never appeared in the Royal Honours List, in spite of three nominations, two of them by me with the backing of Fred's home town MP, Lords Coe and Montagu, even an appeal to the Prince Of Wales himself. Other speedway personalities of far lesser pedigree have MBE attached to their names.

It is exactly sixty-two years ago – too long probably – that in 1953 Fred was crowned World Champion for the second time. And you would think, considering it was Coronation year, the Queen might have seen fit to summon him to Buckingham Palace to show her gratitude for him bringing the honour once more to her kingdom – or is it queendom?.

At the time none of the experts rated his chances. He had scored a useful eight points

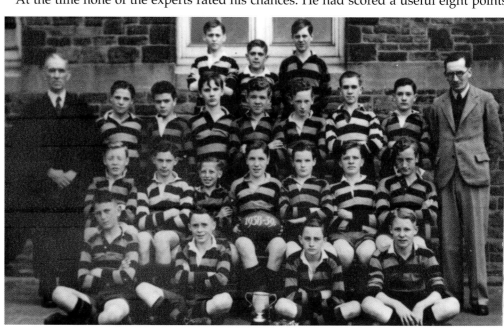

Schooldays. Going back a bit, Fred in the same 1938-39 school rugby team as actor Richard Burton. Fred is in the centre of the top row and Richard is in the second row up, second from the right. Both went on to become big stars in their chosen professsion.

Young man on a mission: Fred about to ride his luck in 1948 when Wembley, displaced from the Empire Stadium by the Olympics, rode at Wimbledon: 'Once you got in the team … you got better and better.'

from six rides in England's 57 – 51 second Test win against Australia at Wembley, his home track, in which his young brother Eric had top scored with a sensational 15 points as reserve. Fred was dumped for the final and deciding match at Birmingham, which England also won.

Yes, Fred the Welshman rode for England. Speedway is like that, isn't it?

At the time, people in the know, who ironically included Fred's Wembley manager Duncan King, were all convinced that Australia's phenomenal Jack Young would become the first to win the world title for a third consecutive time.

This was because Young had confounded the speedway world in 1951 by winning at Wembley while still a Second Division rider with Edinburgh. Jack recalled later that after the meeting Fred scrubbed his back in the Wembley showers – a gentlemanly gesture considering that Jack had just pinched Fred's title. But Fred Williams is like that.

Then Jack had gone on to do what they all said *was* impossible. 'No one can win the World Championship twice,' they said. But he did, with Fred, all smiles, sitting behind him on the Wembley tractor in second place.

Jack's preparation for the big night in 1953 was a trip to the cinema during the afternoon. Fred was out in the Wembley car park practising starts.

The post-war discovery: Wembley manager Alec Jackson proves his faith in Fred was a winner when he presented his young protégé with his first trophy.

And while Fred ended up by getting his world title back, Jack ended up biting the Wembley shale in a vital Heat 20. A win would have put him in a run-off for second place with England's Split Waterman. But he ran over his own foot.

Afterwards, Fred revealed to reporters: 'I practised starting nearly a thousand times in the Wembley Stadium car park. I had the breaks at the start in most of my races – not because I'm a Wembley rider because, believe me, there is no such thing as secret practice on our track.'

The interview was a huge concession to a breathlessly attendant media. He readily admitted that he wasn't fond of talking to the Press, nor did the prospect of signing autographs for fans fill him with eager anticipation.

He said: 'After a meeting I never liked going into the bar to chat to supporters. It was bloody awful to have to sign autographs.'

It is an attitude that, looking back, he came to regret. He confessed: 'I was wrong, I know that now as I have got older.' Until the day he died, three years short of his 90th year, he continually did his best to make up for it. More than half a century on, Fred was always available to do his PR thing for the sport. He was never known to turn down a request to

On his way: Fred, together with four other inexperienced virtual novices, grabbed the chance to go to Australia with Jack Parker's England tourists. They are lined up in Sydney with Fred on the far left, then Dent Oliver, Ron Clarke, Parker, Cyril Roger, Oliver Hart, Bill Kitchen and Howdy Byford. Behind them manager Harry Tovey on the left and pre-war pioneer Australian 'Wizard' Frank Arthur.

Above left:
Learning his trade: Fred getting the hang of international competition in a tough tussle outside the late Norman Clay during the 1949-50 winter tour of Australia.

Above right: *It wasn't all work: Sunning themselves in Brisbane, from left to right Oliver Hart, Fred, Australian photographer Alan Gerrard, Graham Warren, Ken LeBreton, Jack Biggs and Ron Clarke.*

do a personal appearance to further the cause of speedway racing.

Because, as anyone will tell you who knew him in later years, Fred Williams was the quintessential Mr Nice Guy of speedway. There were some, even before the incumbent World Champion Greg Hancock. Fred Williams was one of them.

He did, though, have an on-track mean streak, as every man who ever reached the summit of the sport did. Which is why I called Fred the Jekyll and Hyde World Champion.

His death in early 2013 devastated his myriad of friends and admirers. They had convinced themselves he would go on forever. He was, they said, a credit to the world of speedway racing who wore the crown of World Champion proudly for sixty years and there will not be another like him.

Fred was one of Wembley speedway chief Alec Jackson's typical early post-war discoveries who went on to achieve great things, a dockyard apprentice from Port Talbot who rode grasstrack at weekends with his two brothers, Eric and Ian, both of whom became World Finalists.

Jackson wanted to bring on young British riders, a policy that was really forced upon him by Wembley boss Sir Arthur Elvin – 'the biggest friend speedway ever had'. Elvin had a reputation as being a bit of a martinet and it is said that until Tommy Price won the World Championship, Elvin always addressed him as 'Price'. Only afterwards did he use the more familiar term 'Tommy'.

When the suits shut down Wembley to regular league speedway in 1957 on the death of Elvin, who not only championed the sport throughout his life but had legitimised it as well by opening up his fabulous Empire Stadium to the infant spectacular motorised entertainment in 1929, Fred – who rode for Wembley, and only Wembley – called it quits on his racing career as well.

Left: *The apprenticeship is over: Fred returns from the Australian tour to win the world title in 1950 and is introduced to Earl Mountbatten before the Final at Wembley. In the background Aub Lawson and Jack Parker.*

Right: *Victory parade. The new champion proudly holds the Sunday Dispatch World Championship trophy on the traditional tractor ride.*

With big time speedway starting up again after the war in 1946 Elvin was asked if he would put speedway on again at Wembley. He said he would on condition that he wasn't going to be 'pushed around' again by foreign riders such as Australian Lionel Van Praag who, though bringing huge success to Wembley before the war, Elvin found a somewhat 'difficult' employee.

Elvin did agree to reopen Wembley. He sent for Jackson and told him: 'Get me a team of British riders.' Alec said: 'But there aren't any.' To which Elvin replied: 'Well, make some.'

And that's what Alec did. Wembley advertised for young men who fancied being speedway stars, and rented the Rye House track as a training school. Fred answered the advert and remembered: 'They must have had about 20 speedway bikes – some Excelsiors and some with Wallis frames – a big old Bedford lorry and the bikes were looked after by a couple of the Wembley mechanics, Jim Charnock and Cyril Spinks.'

Elvin made it worthwhile for Alec Jackson and pre-war Belle Vue star Bill Kitchen, who Wembley chose to captain the Lions when the top talent was pooled in 1946, to relocate from their northern homes and take charge of the training sessions at Rye House.

Fred said: 'There were lots of potential speedway riders to choose from because the boys had been racing on Army tracks in Germany and North Africa. I answered the advertisement in *Motorcycle News* and was told to be at Wembley on a particular day. When I arrived there were 20 or 30 others – some of them really rough looking herberts – and we met in

Winning combination. Fred Williams (right) with Cyril Spinks, the wonderful mechanic who looked after the machinery which never broke down.

Team talk: Wembley Lions in a huddle, and Fred, third from left, offers an opinion. To his left Jimmy Gooch and Eric French, to his right Brian Crutcher and Tommy Price.

At home in front of the huge crowds that made the speedway atmosphere of those days so exciting: Fred leading Barry Briggs and Peter Moore of Wimbledon.

the workshops. The bikes were put on the lorry and we all piled into a couple of vans.

'Dicky Case *(the pre-war Australian international)* ran Rye House at the time. It was such an untidy place. There were tin sheets for the safety fence, the track was black cinders, a couple of ancient showers in a tin shed plus a great big box full of leathers, boots, steel shoes and helmets. Nothing fitted, of course, and they said: "Right, fix yourself up." Invariably it was raining. It was winter.

'I'd got quite good on the grass with my old 350cc AJS, but I knew nothing about speedway racing and nothing about being a speedway rider. Anyway, they put me on a 500cc JAP and pushed me off. There was a lot of power and we were all told to ride these things round until we got the feel of it.

Brothers three: the Williams boys, and not all on the same side. Fred, left, and Eric, right, of Wembley and Ian in the colours of Swindon Robins.

'Then they put us through our paces … you've never seen anything like it. They were all a load of nutters, crashing into the fence, blood and gore everywhere. And at the end of it all Alec said was: "We'll let you know."

'After about five or six goes, they gave me a second half race at Wembley – and I'd never seen a speedway meeting. There were these thousands of people in the stadium. When the tapes went up I looped and went over backwards. It was an absolute disaster.

'That was my first meeting at Wembley, but I never, ever looped again.'

Fred recalled walking with Bill Kitchen the length of that intimidating arena from the dressing rooms at one end to the pits at the other. In those days there were regular Wembley crowds of 75,000 – sometimes more – and the waves of sheer adulation that rolled down from the packed terraces to wash over the fans' leather-clad heroes would not disgrace pop idols or film stars today.

Exposure to the vast Wembley crowds immunised Fred against the equivalent of speedway stage fright when it came to major meetings such as World Finals as all around him were falling to pieces with big occasion nerves.

It was an invitation to stay at Bill Kitchen's home after a particularly bruis-

Above left: *World class sporting couple, never far from the Empire Stadium. Wife Pat, an Olympic ice skater, helps Fred keep in shape in the Wembley car park.*

Above right: *High speed Fred after the Astorias Plate trophy at Belle Vue in 1953, the year of his second World title, with those outlandish handlebars very much in evidence again.*

ing day at Rye House that inspired Fred to seek fame and fortune on the speedways. He said: 'Bill was my absolute idol. He had a beautiful house at Wembley and I was shown to a room all to myself. It had a washbasin, and on a shelf above was one of those aftershave spray things.

'The following morning there I was, spraying on this aftershave and thinking: "This is what it could be like for me if I was a speedway rider." And that's what triggered it all off for me.'

A bad ankle injury on the grass meant that Fred was out of action for almost the entire 1947 season. He said: 'You would have thought that Wembley would have written me off then. But they didn't, they kept faith in me and when I was fit again gave me some more second half rides.'

There was speedway every week night in London in those days. Fred said: 'Whenever Wembley were at the other tracks we would be taken there to race against some of their youngsters. This went on for quite a time.

'We had wonderful help from the senior members of the team and Alec Jackson. I always worshipped Bill Kitchen, and you can say what you like about Tommy Price, because he was a ruthless character was Tommy, when he was racing. When he wasn't he was a lovely fellow. A wonderful man. But when you were in a race with him, he did everybody. He had a really mean streak.

'Trevor Redmond used to say that Tommy would give him any gate he wanted as long as Tommy had gate one. But with Split Waterman it got to the stage where there'd be arguments – and Split was a bit of a tiger – so Alec Jackson used to have to decide who would have which gate.

'Wembley loaned me a bike and bought me a new engine. I still got points money from them. We got start money which was £1.50 and £2 a point.

'I was fortunate because Jim Charnock and Cyril Spinks were wonderful mechanics. All the time I raced for Wembley I never broke down – never broke a chain, never dropped a valve. And luck came into it when Bill Kitchen broke an arm at West Ham and soon after that George Wilks broke a leg at Wimbledon. It was an opportunity for people like me. Once you got in the team you got your rides and you got better and better.

'Most teams didn't run like that. People used to think we were a bit ruthless, but Bill Kitchen and Tommy Price were so great to the Wembley riders. There really was a terrific team spirit. And Alec Jackson was brilliant at how he managed the team.

'I didn't have a great deal of contact with Elvin. He used to leave everything to Alec.

Elvin was clerk of the course at Wembley and he used to sit up in the box and watch everything that was going on. If a mechanic came out of the pits with a cigarette in his mouth a message was soon sent down: "Don't let that man anywhere near the Press with a cigarette in his mouth." He was very particular about things like that.

'There is no doubt about it, being attached to a place like Wembley must have helped my career. I was never awestruck by huge crowds because I was used to them. There was such an exciting atmosphere in those days.

'I was a pure novice when I first started at Wembley. Other teams in those days decided this was the right way to do it. Belle Vue had their Dent Oliver and Louis Lawson, West Ham had Howdy Byford and Wally Green, New Cross had Cyril Roger – all of them had only just started.

'At Wembley there was myself, and apart from Bill Kitchen, George Wilks and Tommy Price, who had ridden before the war, the rest of us were unknowns. There was Charlie May, Alf Bottoms, Roy Craighead, Bill Gilbert, Bronco Wilson and Split Waterman.'

Waterman is now the only remaining member of that marvellous early post war Wembley team which won seven League Championships in eight years, two National Trophies, three London Cups and one British Speedway cup. He recalls getting on the wrong side of Jackson on a trip to Belle Vue. He says: 'Fred and I rode there on my BMW motorcycle. When we got there we were knackered and we got into real trouble with Alec.'

Away from the crowds and the adulation Fred, doing his bit for the next generation, explains technique to another aspiring young novice.

World Champion speedway riders used to have their likenesses displayed in the famous Madame Tussaud's Wax Museum in London. A member of Tussaud's staff helps Fred choose from a selection of matching glass eyes.

Jackson's development of young British riders was a three year plan which exceeded all expectations in the first year. Wembley won the National League, the 1946 equivalent of the Elite League. And Price won the British Riders Championship, the season's major individual competition which had temporarily replaced the World Championship.

The record books show that in 1947 Fred Williams scored one single, solitary point for Wembley that season – exactly the same number that, ten years later, a young hopeful named Ivan Mauger scored for Wimbledon.

It took years for Ivan to get the breaks which made the speedway world sit up and take notice. It took Fred Williams one year. They came in 1948, with breaks – to an arm and a lag – for his Wembley team mates Kitchen and Wilks. 'They put me into the team, and I began to score points,' said Fred.

The following year Jack Parker was seeking volunteers for an England team to make a winter tour of Australia, but at a Speedway Riders Assocation meeting none of the so-called star names seemed to want to go.

Four very inexperienced virtual novices sitting together: Howdy Hyford of West Ham, Cyril Roger of New Cross, Dent Oliver of Belle Vue and Fred, shouted: 'We'll bloody well go!' Fred said: 'The next thing we knew we were on the boat.'

Fred learned a lot about speedway on that tour, of that there is no doubt. He came back to England and Wembley and won the World Championship. It had been a mere four year apprenticeship.

It happened on Thursday, 21 September, 1950. He gave much of the credit for his first world title to his mechanic Cyril Spinks. 'Cyril was very, very good,' said Fred. 'All the

Back in the old routine ... almost ... as manager of the 'new' Wembley Lions in the 1970s. From the left they are: Dave Jessup, Bert Harkins, Tim Bungay, Fred, Ove Fundin on the machine, Wayne Briggs, Reidar Eide and Brian Collins.

time I raced at Wembley I never broke down, never broke a chain, never dropped a valve.'

His tactics that night can only be described as shock and awe. All of the sport's elite were there: Tommy Price, Jack Parker, Graham Warren, Jack Young, Aub Lawson, Ronnie Moore, Vic Duggan. The big names didn't bother Fred. His plan was to frighten them all by going out in the first heat and breaking the track record.

'Everything went according to plan. It was a tremendous psychological blow,' said Fred. Second to Fred in that first heat – and on the night – was one of the other virtual unknowns, Wally Green of West Ham who a couple of years before had been riding in the Third Division.

In the following year's final, as outgoing champion, he did poorly, winning only one race. But he vividly remembered his meeting with eventual champion Jack Young in heat 11.

'I made the gate on him,' said Fred. 'But Young was really motoring. For a couple of laps I could hear him trying to come under me, and when that failed, he tried to go round me. It must have been marvellous to watch.

'I was coming down the finishing straight on the third lap and could hear him right behind me. I left it late going into the turn and threw the back wheel out. It hit Youngie and I could hear the clanging and banging.

'I don't think I'm a really nasty person, but I was thinkging: "Well, that's Youngie through the bloody fence." But because we'd got into a bit of s skirmish I was a little wide coing out of the turn – and he came up the inside. He put up with all that and then passed me on the inside. I really did think I'd put him in trouble on that corner.

When they got back to the pits Young approached Fred, who was expecting Jack to have a go at him. But, Fred revealed: 'He just said: "You bastard Willy ... " '

Fred's second title two years later came after he broke all the rules. The night before the Wembley Final he and his wife Pat went clubbing till 4am – not because he was a hell-raiser but because he didn't realise that wild nights on the town were not the way to prepare for winning World Championships.

But he did acknowledge that riding every week at Wembley was a colossal advantage because World finals were always held there then.

After that win Fred thought that as he had been at Wembley a long time and was World Champion, he considered he was worth a bit more than mere points money. He reasoned that the top footballers of the day were going for £35,000, and Split Waterman had been transferred to Harringay for £3,000 plus a percentage of the fee.

'I thought I was worth the same sort of money,' said Fred. 'So I went to Elvin and asked for a transfer too. Sir Arthur – I always called him Sir Arthur – said he wouldn't transfer me. So I said I ought to have some extra cash then. We were pulling in fantastic crowds at

Wembley and all we got was that £1.50 a start and £2 a point.

'He said: "It's against the rules. And I'm chairman of the Speedway Control Board, so you won't get an illegal payment out of me."

'I thought I'd test him and gave him an ultimatum – unless I got some more money I wouldn't race any more. He threatened to have me banned completely, so my one and only attempt at blackmail failed miserably.'

Fred told me: 'The best moments I had in speedway were of course the World championship wins. The worst were riding with my brother Eric. We had some terrible accidents together and he always seemed to come of worst. Eventually I had to refuse to ride with him. When you go into those corners you really don't care about anybody and Eric was always the unlucky one.'

The last time I saw Fred was on the day of the Cardiff Grand Prix in 2012. He had come to support me at a book signing session in the city. He stayed for two hours, chatting freely to fans who came to talk to him. Then, with a protective arm round his wife Pat, they disappeared unrecognised into the crowds.

That night he presented the winner's trophy to the man who was to succeed to the crown he had worn with such distinction so many years ago, Chris Holder.

Fred Williams went about ascending to the top of the speedway world in as dedicated, determined, meticulous and comprehensively prepared way as any World Champion. And in the rough, tough, relentlessly demanding, often cruel, world of speedway you don't win two world titles unless you have a high degree of motorcycling talent.

But he always insisted: 'I never understood why people would think me marvellous. I never considered myself a great World Champion. A fortunate one yes. There were better riders than me in those World Finals that I won.'

A pair of veterans, Fred and the author, dressed up for a special occasion – the World Speedway Riders Association annual dinner as recently as 2012: Fred was WSRA President in 1981 and attended right up to the end.